The Art of the Deal Today

"Finding Capital today is daunting for businesses and the credit markets remain mostly frozen to everyone with the exception of the wealthy and yet innovations in financing business development opportunities are springing up everywhere"

By

Don Allen Holbrook

One of America's Foremost Economic Development Finance Professionals

Table of Contents:

Foreword- How To Facilitate the Obvious
Page 4

Chapter 1- The Gauntlet that Must be run
Page 7

Chapter 2- How to Talk the Talk and Make the Pitch to Local Governments-
Page 23

Chapter 3- Your Local Government Might be Your Best Resource for Financing
Page 30

Chapter 4- Traversing the credit impasse & Frozen Banking Marketplace Today.
Page 38

Chapter 5- Using Friends/Family/Investors
Page 44

Chapter 6- Economic Development Revolving Loan Funds
Page 47

Chapter 7- Using the Small Business Loan & Grant Programs of the US Government
Page 51

Chapter 8- New Market Tax Credit Program
Page 67

Chapter 9- EB5 Immigration Program
Page 71

Chapter 10- Types of Bonds for Small to Medium Businesses
Page 73

Chapter 11- Typical Public Sector Venture Fund Questions for a Business Application for Funding Consideration
Page 78

Chapter 12- The Conclusion for Possible Next Steps
Page 84

Recommended Additional Reading
Page 90

Professional Consulting Services
Page 92

Consultation Questionnaire
Page 95

Glossary of Economic Development Terms
Page 99

Glossary of Useful Financing Terminology
Page 119

About the Author
Page 122

Index
Page 124

Foreword:

How to Facilitate the Obvious

It is a fundamental consideration that government is a servant of the people for the best interests of her people. The fiscal basis of governmental operations is founded on taxing its citizens with reasonable oversight and transparency of their conduct of such operations. Citizens through their representatives or by means of referendum establish tax policies. The distribution of said tax monies is a solemn undertaking; ostensibly, tax policy and distribution of said revenue is purposefully designed to exclusively serve the public's best interest.

An economic developer is a "prime mover," a facilitator of means to an end or facilitator of developing public purpose that will benefit the greatest amount of public positive economic benefits to their representative constituents. As such they are expected to be a liaison extraordinaire, a provocateur of the feasible, a person of specific knowledge interwoven within a general understanding of enterprise, a persona, who above all else, is a person of action. This person is also usually the closest mindset to the entrepreneurs and business owners they seek to serve a rare gem in the collective government cauldron today of bureaucracy.

The raison d'être (purpose of reasoning) of government ingress into the dynamics of economic development is to facilitate employment, broaden the scope of a soundly dependable and sustainable taxable base, and spread the burden of taxation and thus reduce it on her constituents over-all, this is the balance of creating a favorable business investment climate that should promote economic prosperity if done in fiscally prudent balanced governance. Government must while striving to achieve its noted obligations to the electorate mitigate the risk of the people's capital, thus be prudent not to act irresponsibly and thus have the reverse affect of actually increasing the burden on the general public and creating additional or unfundable liabilities. It is such mitigation of risk, all the while, achieving the dynamics of economic development that is the challenging task all towns, cities, counties, provinces, states and even the national governments face in the face of considering how to build a recovery within the global but mostly local economies around the world.

The premise of this book was created with the purpose of designing a 'real world' operational plan of action; a combatants guide of how to analysis and decipher possibilities presented, establish project specific criteria, create an operational gauntlet, and utilize the power of persuasion in the interest of consensus.

There has been a paradigm shift in the United States over the last couple of years towards bigger government as a solution for economic development or economic recovery. The involvement of the central government in such concepts is not something that should be done without considerable discourse. Setting precedents for putting taxpayer monies at risk is a dangerous slippery slope.

There is no doubt that government can and should play a role in the recovery process in particular in creating the right business climate for market makers and investments to begin to flow once again into projects that create jobs, increase and enhance the tax base for governance and diversify and create new market based opportunities within all levels of the economy. In the end it is always the local economic decisions that have the economic initiative that create opportunity and it is usually the higher levels of public policy with regard to business climate that require local level adjustments in order to maintain some modicum of reality for continued or renewed economic growth. These various levels of government are not efficient in their dealings with each other and thus great disparity exists within the over-all market place from city to city, state to state and country to country.

This calls into question the manner in which and under what conditions should if any tax payer monies be placed at risk and if so why and how do they reduce liabilities and get surety for such actions? The risk and reward of such considerations is a heady matter. Growing government involvement is not a panacea for assuring success in such endeavors and could just turn into a boondoggle that consumes taxpayer monies unnecessarily if not approached under the right mindset. Running these gauntlets requires a savvy approach and getting into such endeavors should only be done under the right market based conditions. This book will lay out a plan for approaching a market-based approach to engaging a balance public private partnership approach to capitalizing economic development investments in this new era.

Chapter 1:

The Gauntlet that must be Run

Today the competition for capital is intense and it places even more pressure on public sector governmental and quasi-governmental entities to engage in catalyst type projects to ignite and/or renew their local economies. The temptation to meddle and tinker with ideas of just how to best incentivize the private sector into investing into economic development type projects is as old as capitalism itself. Today people seem to think that each crisis we face is unique and the first of it's kind and nothing is further from the truth we have numerous lessons throughout history about governments responding to crisis of all types, including bubbles which are themselves as old as capitalism. None-the-less, the mixing of public and private sector capital to achieve acceptable outcomes from the perspective of various levels of government is an inevitable engagement.

Therefore, in this book what we will discuss is how best to run the proverbial gauntlet of risk and reward with regard to public sector funding so that the outcomes justify the engagement and involvement of business climate incentives in the name of economic development.

Since the use of public capital is a serious matter we must take a hard look at how best to engage such capital so that the gauntlet can be navigated with a high degree of scrutiny and transparency that will make such engagements accountable to the general public. In all cases there needs to be a practical approach that develops the use of criteria for such investments that can assist in avoiding transactions that would otherwise put such public capital into non-recoverable investments. Bad investments would erode the public trust given to governmental agencies as the representatives of their financial interests. Thus running the gauntlet is as much a science as it is an art of skilled but learned practices that improve the odds of such investments being successful.

The Audit of Public Purpose Leadership-Locales is only as good as their leadership and any community can prevail in economic growth!

One of the first criteria when considering the entire climate for creating public private partnerships is the actual capacity of the general public for being engaged in such activities in the first place. Most private sector firms miss the mark totally on this issue until it is too late and they have inadvertently placed too much financial trust in their public sector partner that cannot actually effectuate the financial outcome that they had hoped for. The biggest cause for such misplaced trust is the complete break down on doing as much due diligence on the public side of the ledger as their public sector requires of their private sector partners. While it may appear that we are discussing a financial review we are not, that will come in the next chapter. When private sector firms seek to adjoin with a public sector partner it is essential to their success that they understand the actual connections to the public leadership with regard to the structure of the political jurisdiction they are considering, as well as the actual experience and acumen of the elected and appointed staff they will be partnering with.

There are varying forms of administrative management styles of many different forms of economic development and other public sector agencies engaged in the capitalization of business investments to create jobs, increase the tax base of the jurisdiction and usually to diversify the local economy. The enabling laws behind each agency differ widely and give a wide variety of powers and limitations of powers as to how they have to conduct themselves on any area of activities. If there is a question of whether the agency has the power to actually conduct the business transaction in question there is even a process for determining that. Doing an audit of the powers and thus the parameters and limitations of the public partner is essential prior to getting into a public private partnership.

In addition, to the actual boundaries of public sector involvement in these type capitalization projects there is also the need to audit and understand the motivation of their leadership for doing so. What is their history of success or failure and/or do they actually have any experience at these type matters. What is the political motivation for the elected leadership to conduct such consideration and how could this change over the timeline for good or bad and under what pressures from the public that might be foreseeable? These are the types of questions one should ask themselves of their public sector partners prior to committing to a major investment that depends on the surety of such knowledge staying in the project until it is brought to a successful outcome. Nothing can blow a project onto the rocks of a stormy economic sea, than a change in the political mood that disavows their involvement prior to sustainable operational achievement or worse yet, that refuses to complete the original terms of the transaction due to a change in the perception by their constituents. Even public sector agencies gets buyers remorse and rethink their involvement in risky or perceived poor general public acceptance and/or approval of such projects at some point.

This chapter will discuss those considerations and steps that can be taken to protect both the public and private sector from engaging in a project that lacks enough political will and/or legal allowance for reaching critical mass. Understanding the realistic constraints of each partner is critical in achieving a successful partnership.

Public Solvency (Capacity for risk & reward)

In today's highly leveraged and over-debt burdened society government is no different than the citizens she is meant to serve and the businesses in the economy, she has financial problems with cash flow, debt service and additional demand for services with insufficient resources to pay for the burden of her legacy costs in many cases.

One of the most common mistakes in considering how or if to create and then participate in a public-private partnership endeavor is understanding and assessing the financial capacity of the public sector just as they will need to do the same on the private sector partners.

To make the assumption that just because an elected body of government agrees to a set of financial terms and conditions and binds themselves to be obligated to pay for their portion, does not mean that they ultimately have the cash flow to do so. This can be especially true in these times, where cities derive a huge amount of the projected income and thus already obligated debt services based on their historical and projected cash receipts from things such as sales tax, licenses, permits and property taxes. As times get economically challenging these revenues may decline significantly. Evidence of basing the public sector fortunes on these strategies and thus a house of cards is all around us in the news today.

Government does possess the unique ability to create forced financial solutions, called new or increased taxes to handle such matters, but doing so sets a huge chain of other potentially harmful side effects into play. It is for this reason that governments usually if prudent take the raising of taxes as a very grave and in most cases a last option of choice to solving their financial matters.

In establishing a well-oiled and sustainable public-private partnership that has adequate financial wherewithal to survive economic downturns and flourish and reduce obligations when operating properly during normal or good times takes good strategic planning. There is no cookie cutter approach to designing such a partnership infrastructure on the public side, but understanding the tools they have available to them is a good first step.

In this chapter we will discuss how to review and understand the financial capabilities of the public sector partner and how to think outside of the box to leverage those tools and create some new ones in some cases to assist in securing the capital to invest in catalyst projects.

Developing the Right Collaborative Mindset- Attitude is Everything!

Once you have gotten your mind around the political disposition and motivation, you understand how the public sector jurisdiction is organized and lawfully what their constraints are for operations and decision making and you know their financial capacity and approach to solving public investments, you now are better suited for how to approach designing the public-private partnership.

The private sector rather than approaching this as a corporate welfare opportunity has their own unique set of challenges to prepare their own mindset to think of this as a unique opportunity for a joint venture. Treating the public sector partner as just that a full fledged and thus invested partner and equity player in the deal is the first must have requirement for a proper mindset.

Involving the public sector in a matter that is not necessary is foolish, cumbersome and frankly not good for our underlying business climate as a matter of national economic wellbeing. You do not want to knowingly contribute to the undermining of our country by being a part of the problem, but rather these type opportunities should be approached as creating solutions that will raise our economic state of competitiveness and increase jobs, tax base and diversify the economy because of your efforts.

Therefore taking on a public-private partnership raises the stakes for you as a US citizen to think about the greater good and not just your own best interests. You would not like paying your own tax dollars that you worked so hard to contribute to the various governments to be squandered or foolishly invested and lost and thus raise your tax bill even higher the next year.

The use of public funds requires a higher bar or level of performance and surety than the private sector has for investment considerations. It also requires absolute transparency, accountability and understanding of the "If Not But For," clause of calling the public sector into action in projects.

In this chapter I will discuss how the proper mindset involves several layers of pre-designed protocols that should be adhered to in order to create a healthy and functional mindset to traverse these unique waters of economic opportunity and peril simultaneously.

Validation of Concepts- how do you know what you don't know?

Once a project has passed the initial merits of this sounds like a good idea and it seems to fit the desired outcomes that all parties believe would suit their mutual interests, we step into the higher level tier of proof of concept and validation of market reality. This is the stage where the stakes get exponentially higher and where a good bit of misconceptions can occur if not managed and handled with care and prudence. It is essential in this stage that we always consider the mindset of our partners and how such due diligence information may affect their actions and opinions either positively, negatively, unrealistically or prematurely rather than as a course of deliberation and testing of facts versus other best practices, existing experiences and practical knowledge of others that have trodden this course and navigated these waters before.

In the proof of concept stage the public sector needs to have adequate assurance that the due diligence studies are being conducted by unbiased and expert resources. These experts should not be singing for their supper... to further their work efforts for additional employment. The best approach is to make sure there is a proactive statement about the outcome must be capable of saying "No Go," or "Yes" or even a conditional "Yes or Maybe" as part of the requirements. Such due diligence needs to take a look at this from worst case, best case; likely outcomes based on historical assumptions and hybrid "What If?" considerations. Applying market conditions and financial realities then to such considerations should be a carefully vetted modeling approach and again conducted by an outside unbiased source to assure the best knowledge and oversight to such findings.

Since the public sector is involved in this process the outcomes should not be skewed with that prospect. In other words the "What if They weren't" consideration should be the best course of consideration.

There are many pitfalls to this stage. First and foremost is the rush or exuberance to want to find out or verify your prejudice on the matter. The public sector is no different, especially in an election year. The politicos will want to get out the good news or potential for good news in many cases way too prematurely.

Remember one expert opinion does not make it right... getting other perspectives is essential to designing and implementing a good project and then to get it to sustainable operations is another entirely different matter. Interviewing and understanding failures is just as important as understanding and learning about successes in these cases.

In this chapter we will discuss the best approach to validating the proof of concept from a market perspective and getting comfortable with the costs associated with succeeding.

Designing the Instruments of a Public-Private Partnership for small & medium Businesses use to grow their capacity market share

The choice of utilizing a public sector and/or quasi public sector partner has many pitfalls, but it also has many fruits of opportunities. The creation of unique financial tools is something that can be achieved by way of legal design when using a public partner. This can be done as part of a local decision already allowable under state charter, the creation of special state legislation to enable such special circumstances and/or the exclusive design of a exclusionary business case in order to get market penetration and sustained market share... in other words a public sector partnership can for all intensive purposes create a monopoly for some justified reasoning if they so desire. They are not necessarily held to the same standard as the rules for competition in the private sector. This does not mean that I am advocating for such situations and/or that the public sector would agree to conduct their affairs in that manner.

The creation of hybrid instruments with the perceived value of the good faith backing of the public sector does create some unique opportunities for attracting funding of projects. Just the addition of a public sector partner will in many cases create better trust that such projects will be successful and thus pay back their investors. It also many times can get more favorable interest rates and tax treatment if there are public designed incentives for investors to participate.

Some of the primary considerations in designing such instruments is how much should it participate, how will it be justified, and what is the exit strategy for the public sector if any and at what point does it occur?

In this chapter we will discuss the considerations that can be given to create a criteria for building such instruments and how they can be used to successfully position a project to attract private sector investment.

Attracting Private Sector Participation

There is no better validation of concept than the willingness of the private sector to pony up financial funds in support of the project, with or without public sector participation. In the sense that if it just makes economic sense then the risk will be mitigated by the desire for making this into a profitable venture. The vast majority of projects fit into this category already. Private groups and investors believe in a concept and put their funds at risk to prove it and bring it to market... thus we have capitalism.

The new models of public participation in private risk projects is not new at all, it has been around since the inception of capitalism. China, Japan, Netherlands, Denmark, Sweden, Singapore, Hong Kong, Switzerland all have models that have used similar concepts for varying degrees of investments into industries deemed in the best interest of their governments to spawn new private sector industries.

The attraction of the private sector and the assignment of the most appropriate degree of risk to them is the best arbiter of validation of concept and market realities of reasonable risk. It is for this matter that finding the appropriate private sector partners with the necessary solvency and financial expertise and depth is critical to the success of well-designed public-private partnerships.

In this chapter we will discuss the possibilities that might be considered in what type of private sector partners to focus your efforts upon and what criteria might be used to peak their interest in your projects.

Risk & Reward Balance of Power and Struggle for Deal Equilibrium

The desire for reward, glory, power and profits are all similar attributes of the human spirit. They are also present in public sector; private sector and non-profit activities are just expressed sometimes quite differently.

Profits in the private sector are a good thing. That means the investment has funds to either reinvest in the further growth of the business and expansion of their markets or to pass on as dividends to their shareholders (the risk takers). Profits in the public sector can and normally are looked at in a different mindset. They are unused funds collected from the public, a carry forward. How often do you see the government say, Oops we collected too much and here is your rebate? Not very often. In fact, the public sector may take a traditional mindset of practicing the age old, "use it or lose it" approach. In other words if we don't spend all we have, even if it is not necessary they will cut us back next year. So they tend to try to spend all their budgeted funds mostly as they had predicted they would be required. But some governments program these type funds to special projects to address such things as catalyst projects and public-private partnership investments. The non-profit sector simply refers to these profits as surplus funds, and doesn't have the same philosophy or mindset necessarily as government, unless in some cases the source of the funds was originated as public taxpayer monies from tax collections.

This approach to profits is essential in understanding the risk reward mentality of dealing with non-private sector sources of funding.

The risk of public sector investors is much more tolerable to risk than the private sector in many cases because their attitude is less prone to see it as the loss of their hard earned monies. That does not mean they do not take such considerations highly serious or without great regard for the considerations of whether these type investments should be made. The criteria for reward are far different than those of the private sector and even than the non-profit sector.

The reward in the private sector is something we all recognize much easier, profits, riches and lucrative increased economic status and lifestyle attainment. These are identified in our own American credo as the pursuit of happiness, the attainment of the proverbial American Dream.

The reward in the non-profit sector is usually linked to sustaining their mission, accomplishing a defined set of tasks that drive their mission, objectives and fulfill the purpose of their organizational focus in the world and the communities and constituents they seek to serve.

The sense of reward in the public sector is an extension of the ethos practiced in the non-profit sector but to a much more refined basis. It is normally linked to the creation of jobs or preservation of jobs in many cases today, increasing and/or restoring the tax base to healthy sustainable levels adequate enough for them to serve their greater mission to meet the expectations of their constituents, and to diversify their local economy, under the assumption that diversification makes it less prone to a narrow focus economic down turn that wrecks too much havoc and chaos within their community and thus drives down their over-all quality of life through the loss of economic opportunity.

In this chapter I will discuss how to design and consider the rewards and economic justification for creating a basis for the public sector to consider becoming a risk-taking partner in a public-private partnership catalyst project investment opportunity. Why they would choose to do so and how to design your rewards to merit their involvement. How to create an equitable balance of power for risk versus reward that balances private sector needs and expectations with private sector requirements, desired outcomes and reality-based expectations, is an essential piece of knowledge.

Answering the "If Not But For" Question Honestly

Perhaps one of the most misunderstood concepts today in the engagement of government within traditional private sector affairs whether in banking, finance & equity markets, manufacturing, energy, infrastructure and other economic development activities is the basis for involving the government in the first place.

In the olden days (1980's and 1990's or prior) we used to practice an age-old concept called the "If Not But For," clause. The meaning was used to convey the consideration allegedly given to involving public sector funds into a private sector transaction to make it meet the needs of the private sector taking the primary risk. The theory goes like this, if not but for the involvement of the government in this project by creating or investing the disclosed special conditions and in many cases funds or business climate stimulus the project would not get funded by the private sector and thus be possible to bring to fruition. However, inventing cause and justification is human nature and we have taken great pain in creating really resourceful means of conveying the perception for the basis for such needs. Entire consulting practices have been birthed to address them and legions of lobbying special interest groups practice singing the virtues of this in every hall of government around the world.

In the end, it is my opinion that given such rampant abuse of this clause only lends credence to the need to adequately address it in the new public-private partnerships that will be birthed in this century. Paying honest attention to the basis for when and if to engage a government that is by many peoples assessment becoming too involved in private matters and thus eroding their confidence in the markets being able to once again perform adequately with the right balance of oversight, regulation and accountability and thus surety for those using them is more essential then the extension and building of a more robust nanny state central government or local governments.

In some circles within the economic development arena there is a call to create a more robust set of standards addressing the "If Not But For," clause by having it directly inserted into public investments and well defined to the general public, as to why and what the benefits are going to be in very transparent and clear terms. The intent is to reduce the ability for such decisions to be made too lightly and/or for those making such decisions to claim plausible denial of knowledge of all the facts.

Given what many feel will be a rebound effect from the current big-government reaction to the economic meltdown of 2008 through today, it is recommended that prudent practitioners of public-private partnerships begin to design for these considerations and meet those criteria voluntarily as a show of forward thinking and a well balanced mindset for the cause and call to action of engaging the public sector in transactions.

In this chapter I will discuss how to design and create a well thought out "If Not But For" clause with documented criteria recommendations on how to justify such investments. In addition, I will discuss holding all parties accountable to meet their stated objectives with milestones and reasonable and transparent outcomes that can be measured and reported to the general public. Building a working relationship of trust and transparency with the general public should be seen as a positive outcome of designing these tools and restoring public confidence in their governance if possible could be a well deserved intangible windfall from a proper designed "If Not But For," clauses in projects.

Designing a Fair and Equitable Exit Strategies

Just as investors seek a recognized methodology for how to reap their rewards, liquidate their investments and decide how much risk to maintain in an investment for how long, so should the public sector.

Public-private partnerships are not designed to last forever in most cases. They were conceived to address the lack of capacity for the private sector to take on a risk and/or special project given the current conditions and economic uncertainties pertaining to those project investment opportunities. So in many cases these public-private partnerships are referred to as catalyst projects that spur action in the form of joint investment, involvement and mitigation of upfront and on-going operational risks. These investments should not be undertaken if at the point the public sector investment runs out the validity of the operation runs aground as well. If such investments cannot achieve critical mass in a reasonable time frame and thus become sustainable, perhaps the investment was never founded on real market realities and probably should not have been undertaken in the first place.

Given the concept of being truly catalyst projects, then we should design a very well defined exit strategy that rewards the risk takers in this case the public sector for their involvement. I would argue that just avoiding risk for the private sector and getting public monies paid back is insufficient reasoning to garner the use of public funds, and/or special favors that translate to increased profits for the private sector.

Therefore designing an adequate reward and then exit strategy to fund the reward is essential in the initial stages of the public-private partnership construction of the relationship. Many communities have very lofty goals for their quality of life amenities, education, economic development infrastructure, performing & visual arts, tourism & recreational opportunities that can be considered as possible benefactors to such public-private partnerships.

In this chapter I will discuss some possible considerations that might meet the call to action of public assistance and risk in projects and meet the general publics idea of public benefits for doing so.

If You Build-it Will they Come?

This is not a Hollywood movie, but the risk and thus potential for reward could be well characterized by the movie's plot and concept. If you choose to step out and do something unique and different that engages a much higher degree of risk and shifting of existing operational paradigms within your community, it does not come without true risk of failure and the realistic opportunity for reward. The answer to the question of "If We Build This Will They Come?" cannot only be surmised and pontificated upon in advance… there is no other way through to the answer other than taking that leap of faith into the unknown void of probable and potential outcomes and riding the currents to the inevitable outcome to answer the question.

In this book, I will attempt to make the decision making process that you may want to consider clear and concise as to many aspects of how to best judge how and if you should recommend to be involved in such projects and if so under what potential terms and conditions and then how best do you serve your purpose and then how and when do you get out of harms way and let the market carry it forward into the sustainable practice of capitalism? These questions and many others will be addressed as part of this new credo of how to conduct yourself successfully in designing a project well versed in "The Art of The Deal Today."

Chapter 2:
How to Talk the Talk and Make the Pitch to Local Government:

The search for capitalization as by now you have ascertained in my opinion should consider and employ the involvement and engagement of your local or quasi governmental resources that have been charged with being the Paladins of your local economy... those folks we fondly refer to as economic developers. This enlistment of their support is not something that they might always naturally have the vision and acumen to recognize at first glance. By their very nature they have been born of political and thus somewhat questionable birthright. What I mean by that is they are constantly fighting for recognition and validation of the need for their own very existence with their very parents that spawned them. Therefore, they are always seeking to find projects and influential people that have needs they can cater to in order to further their own needs to prove the need for their paychecks. The reason I bring this to your attention in this chapter is that if you are to engage them and get what you need and want from them you have to play to their underlying needs they themselves have to prove justification to their parents (Local Government and Business Leaders) that they are needed and necessary.

First let us look at your project needs from how we can build the political willful support from the politicians that you need so that the economic developers will pay special attention to being attentive to your needs as well.

Politicians by nature are creatures of very interesting charisma. They are normally ego driven and use the justification that their intentions are to serve the best interest of their constituents, and they will spin everything to sound like that at least in their sound bytes. Just understand that at their core they can be like chameleons changing directions, support and acknowledgment of their intentions as often as the wind changes directions. This also means normally they will do so to serve their own purposes of propagating their own survival in office. To be successful this means as a businessperson you must understand that at the core level of human trust in the concept of their word is their bond that statement has very little credible value that you can bank upon. Secondary to this is that even if you have it in writing they will either try to craft any written document to have some sense of plausible denial. Meaning that it can be taken in another context if they need to shift their position due to some general public perceptions that might blow back on their own political survival. Your purposes of course is to get what you get in writing from them as simple and clean as possible and use it to your own best advantage understanding the limited value it might have in actual definitive value. The power of the document you get from politicians is best used as a persuasive tool with their indirect minions the economic developers and local administrative staff of the governmental jurisdictional bodies they have influence with.

It is for this reason that early on in my engagement I look for what I call the gaging of Political Will to support a business project and I ask for a demonstration of that support with a letter of support from the various political elected representatives. I always ask for the Mayor, maybe a City or Town Council person, County Commissioner, State Representative, State Senator, and even a Congressman if possible. This stack of supporters if arranged and written up carefully can demonstrate a keen sense of political acumen on your part to the economic developers. They can now see the intrinsic value supporting your project may have in building a platform that furthers their own secondary goals of proving their own worth to those they serve for income.

The use of these letters and how you get them as to be tied in most cases to an emotional almost Apple Pie America theme that is so obvious that no red blooded American could say no to supporting your business endeavor.

It is not our position in this early stage to debate the merits of your business, the validity of your concept, or the feasibility of your financial situation as to whether this support should be given. It is being given for a far simpler matter and that their support should not be unreasonably withheld because of the merits we are putting forth.

Here is an example;

"My company is considering (expanding, opening, relocating) to your community because we believe the business climate in your locale (city name, county, etc.) may offer the right economic, political and market sensibility that will allow my company to become very profitable and successful by making a decision to invest in your location. Over the next few months we will be working with your local and state economic development folks to make sure that in fact the due diligence as to this decision supports our initial consideration instincts to this regard.

Our company if we make this final decision will be making a significant investment into your locale of time, money and resources that will once we are operational generate much needed new jobs, eventually new tax base, and significant direct, indirect and induced long-term economic impact in your local, state and our national economy. Furthermore, our presence in your locale will assist in your current economic development plan to diversify your local economy, build competitive new industries and continue to build the most competitive business climate that will sustain and grow the workforce of your region with economic opportunities well into the future.

We would like a letter of support from you that indicates your willingness to demonstrate your support for our company making the decision to invest in your area and further assist you in achieving the stated goals of your constituents."

It would be a rare politician that would not jump on that bandwagon to support a pitch letter written like this. Yet nothing we have said in this letter is definitive or finalized. Even better we have not narrowed down the chance that we are not looking at other areas to consider what they are willing to do in order to get our attention. This can be used in our final site location decision to our own best needs.

Now for example, I can say to another community well I have considerable political support for our project being demonstrated from this other community (normally we pick one that is a natural competitor for these purposes.) We are not lying our statement is true.

With this in hand we ask them to demonstrate their own level of support... only this time we add just a bit more language to our political willingness show of support to add in few key additional features that we can then use again with our other suitors.

Example:
We use the same language we already used in our initial pitch but we add in the following small caveats.

"In order for us to make the determination of our best location it is imperative that your local economic development officials provide us with definitive proof of market feasibility, suitable site and facility choices with the most affordable and best purchase and/or turnkey lease terms and the availability of adequate financial capital within your market to finance our project. In addition, we will need to see that our investment will be economically profitable to our bottom line and produce the right economic outcomes that will cause the investment to build the support of our own shareholders and potential new investors. Once this business case can be established we look forward to working with you closely for the groundbreaking date and opening ribbon cutting so that our efforts can be visible to your community and of course we will gladly denote that without your support and involvement none of this would have been possible."

As you can see I am building the case for narrowing them down without yet getting specific as to what we are asking them to do. Once we have these letters in hand we can then begin our conversation with the various economic development players from a position of strength. They see that their parents want them to assist us and the needs are fairly well stated in our letter to their parents... and we then give those broad statements our more definitive clarity in this conversation. Cautiously though, as we need to slowly lure them into having to make the case for their need to do this work and provide us with what we consider to be acceptable proof of these concepts. Why is this important you may say? Well, they will normally take the position of saying you need to bring this proof to them... and we want just the opposite. We want them to expend their own resources on things that help your business build its business plan and business case that will have financial market credibility. Thus reducing your own out of pocket expenses and creating some equitable value for your business at the expense of your local government. Here is where you must understand that I do not consider this to be despicable or underhanded at all, in fact I believe it is their mission to do just what you are asking them to do. Economic developers are constantly spouting about the facts that their locales are the greatest places to invest, work, live, recreate and the list goes on. Each of them is trained to be a professional cheerleader to this effect. What you are doing is asking them to "Prove It to Me." What better way than to put them through this exercise, which in the end, results in a company being announced that will create jobs, tax base, economic diversification, and a healthier local economy.

Now, the conversation can be driven to get some real results from the local economic development folks that will drive to this being achieved or not, but if it is not possible at least both parties know they have factual basis for why, and the private business is not wasting time, money and resources on empty promises made from marketing pitches by paid cheerleaders (economic developers) that are merely signing for their supper (maintaining their paychecks and organization financial support) through using such projects as half-empty reasons to further support their efforts. They are in fact earning their keep in a way that is significant and beneficial to both parties. I actually call this reverse engineering the investment capitalization process for funding success. The reason being that along with your public partners as you reach impasses or obstacles and you create realistic work around solutions each time you get closer to the final result, getting the business funded with terms and conditions that are acceptable to the business and the public sector partner. In addition, inevitably once you get down to an acceptable term sheet there will be the ultimate "If Not But For" support clause built into the term sheet by the private sector funding sources that requires the public sector to perform certain favors in order for the investment to be made. This is exactly what you want. Now they either have to put up or shut up. If they can't perform, then you know the requirements of the private sector and can use this to find a community that is willing to give those special conditions (economic incentives) in order to get the jobs and investment promised from the private sector business, which now is backed by legitimate funding sources.

It is for this reason that I engage in this entire process and why I believe in the eventual outcome that will result in a great business project that is capitalized and ready for prime time.

It is important to also remember that the rejection of these terms of the private investment funding can create considerable media negativity for the politicians that gave that initial support to the project, thus their pressure on the economic developers and the staff to accept the terms and find acceptable solutions will increase your own business leverage. This does not guarantee success, but it does increase the probability of success exponentially in my opinion.

29

Chapter 3:

Your Local Government Might be Your Best Resource for Financing
"The 7-Step Process of Soliciting Public Funds for your Business"

1.) What are you trying to finance? - You must decide for what purposes are you trying to raise cash and what are you willing to give up in the attainment of these funds? Typically there are several desired purposes and some of them are not usually very acceptable unless pre-negotiated prior to the application for the funding consideration. Those usually acceptable purposes are as follows;

   a.) Building and/or remodeling or purchasing new facilities, equipment and fixtures.
   b.) Expanding your product and/or services into new growth niches or markets
   c.) Paying for the professional services to expand your business and attain adequate financing including site infrastructure, site improvements, site engineering, legal and other site location associated professional fees
   d.) Purchasing new or additional raw materials and/or inventory for resale or value added production

2.) Myths or at Least Difficult to Obtain Uses of Capital- while there are some very rare exceptions most public sources of capital generally do not invest and/or provide debt financing for the following;

   a.) Working Capital to pay partner's salaries or key employees such as owners or stockholders.

b.) Merger and Acquisition funding however there are some exceptions here if the company being acquired is going to relocate those assets and employment operations to the community and state providing the funding.
c.) Paying for business plans, market analysis or financing consultants unless in some cases the financing comes with an executable term sheet and those expenses are wrapped into the face amount of the over-all financing. Generally the public agencies prefer performance based consulting fees as eligible costs for reimbursement and/or financing with their funding
d.) Site control or options on property while obtaining the financing package. However, there are some exceptions to this if the project is sizeable and from a company with strong performance operations and financials over the past 3-5 years.
e.) Grants to fund speculation or concepts is very rare but there are some exceptions when a community has a strong desire to diversify their own economic base and sees your project as an avenue to that means... these are referred to by me as Catalyst projects... projects that produce a desired windfall even if they fail to meet the original intent of undertaking the funding.

3.) Making the pitch for Public Funding needs to be organized and does cost money. You will typically need the following items to get through the process of utilizing some form of public and/or quasi public debt or equity funds to achieve your business capitalization needs;

- A.) Business Plan (up to date and backed up by credible third party professional opinions from the niche industry you are in as a company).
- B.) Existing Financials normally of 3 years along with Tax Returns
- C.) A Pro-forma Business Case based on financial projections that are acceptable to most General Accounting Procedures. Should be prepared by a CFO or certified accountant or qualified investment banker.
- D.) Statement of the Sources and Uses of Cash that relate to the business case. This should provide great detail and include cost estimates by third parties when applicable.
- E.) Market Validation- which is an independent third party unbiased expert or group of experts that conclude that your business is valid and makes sense given the current market conditions and stated opportunities that have been made in your business plan.
- F.) Cost Verification such as Site Control, Site improvements, Site and/or facility inspections for financing concerns such as Soils, historical significance, environmental issues, zoning, etc.
- G.) A list of incentives that can be provided that can improve the outcomes or likelihood of success for the project, such as Tax Abatement, Tax reimbursement, site or facility leveraged and/or equity contributions, workforce tax credits, inventory exemption tax approval, permit fees being waived, impact fees being waived, and state or other local government financing and/or equity grant participation. This list is the reduction of risk on the front end by mutual or shared risk by other parties not directly involved in the company's

ownership such as the local government, county government, state/provincial governments and sometimes the federal governments. This reduces the over-all operating costs and in many cases the start-up costs of the new operations and thus improves the investors ROI and ROE and reduces some of the upfront risks to the private sector.

H.) Economic Impact Statement is the political tool used to tell the public sectors story to their constituents for why they are taking this risk. Remember that most political risk is taken for the obvious stated reasons of making the politicians look good and secondarily to achieve their stated mission. If you think those are reversed then you are in my opinion naïve. The economic impact statement will focus normally on the following issues that politicians and economic developers seem to thrive upon. Those are job to be created and that includes direct (those the company will employ), indirect (those jobs that will be supported, retained or grown secondarily within the market due to the payroll and operations of this company's investment that are sustainable-ongoing) and induced temporary jobs... jobs that will be short lived over some period of time such as construction and other jobs usually in the first 12-24 months but that will sunset after that. These are then measured for their impact on the community both in the first year, first five years and then on a cumulative basis projected to match the public risk period (usually 10-20 years). This analysis should include the positive impact of the company's operations on the tax climate for the local, county and state as supporting evidence that can be used in the pursuit of funding support from all of those additional capital sources during this process.

4.) Identifying Capital Sources- This can be a very time consuming and in many cases expensive process. There are some very significant factors that most websites cannot explain in enough detail to adequately address the real process of successfully running the gauntlet to obtain public sector financial funding for your business. For example the ability to combine many different sources of capital or not is a critical experience based piece of information that most traditional information brokers cannot explain unless they have had actual experience in the matters. Additionally understanding what motivating factors drive positive decisions to support or provide financial funding from the perspective of the community leadership and political infrastructure is usually super important in the pursuit of these types of funds. While very few consultants will take on such projects in an at-risk mode or pay if you achieve the results due to so many intangibles that they cannot control. However, a proper performance based consultant can reduce those costs by creating a reasonable scale of fees to be paid upon attainment of milestones in many cases. In addition, some performance-based consultants will lobby that the local government pay those fees on your behalf or rebate those fees to the company once the company achieves financing. These become part of the local economic development incentive package if this is agreed to as part of the public-private memorandum of understanding MOU.

5.) Additional information and/or expenses you may incur if you choose to raise some or all of this money in the form of equity from private individuals. First and foremost you must look to see what type of restrictions apply on the type of corporate entity you are using and within the state you are registered. Then that formula needs to be applied to the investor capital solicitation package, which is usually called a Private Placement Memorandum (PPM). Creating a PPM is not simple but it can be simplified and deeply reduced in cost by following some short-cuts, such as purchasing a valid off the shelf downloadable PPM from a business document legal service online and then having your CPA and Attorney make any necessary modifications to this document. Creating one from scratch is normally not necessary as there are so many examples inventoried now you can usually find an example that fits your need.

6.) If the PPM or state requirements are too cumbersome or can't provide enough financing to address your equity needs you have a combination of choices generally;
- A.) Seek the advice of a qualified investment banker
- B.) Start making pitches to venture capital and/or angel investors or funds of such folks
- C.) Change the rules by innovating- there are many delisted public companies that are available for purchase from the Over The Counter (OTC) or sometimes called Pink Sheets. These funds are generally not followed by Broker Dealers that normally deal in high value publicly traded companies but none-the-less there is a positive brand for having a publicly traded company, stock symbol and the appearance of financial regulatory transparency. These firms can sometimes be purchased and repurposed for around $100,000 USD or less for your needs. This then allows you to sell your stock to many more than the restricted private offering but it comes with a cost of accounting and

reporting annually that can be $10,000 USD or more in many cases just for compliance. It does give a creative and innovative entrepreneur some additional angles and funding flexibility and may increase your attractiveness to the public sector and/or quasi-public sector economic development organizations that your company may still want to seek for part of their funding and/or defrayment of business costs in this endeavor.

7.) Assembling the entire array of products, documents and support materials is a daunting task and even more formidable when you are also running the actual business enterprise. It is for this reason that I highly recommend the use of an experienced Master Consultant in the Site Location & Economic Development Public Policy arena to coordinate and advise the company or entrepreneur through this process. A Master Consultant can normally assess the validity of the business and whether they feel comfortable undertaking the representation by a short 15-30 minute preliminary free interview and/or consultation. Remember their questions will normally focus on the intended use of the funds, where you intend to make the investment, what the jobs and other economic impacts will be on the benefiting community and the size, scope and nature of the business as well as the acumen and validity of their perception of the initial business case. If they feel most obstacles can be overcome by their own experience they will ask you if you would like them to send you a retainer agreement, where the terms of their representation (fees, outcomes and disclaimers of those services will be outlined.)

Chapter 4:

Traversing the credit impasse and Frozen Banking Marketplace Today.

With bank lending figures continuing to fall, Hundreds of thousands of entrepreneurs are looking for alternative sources of funding to get their business off the ground and restore hope and income to their future prospects. If you're in this category, this chapter may provide you with some knowledge to navigating some of the basic tools and options at your disposal if you are willing to work and innovate in your credit search for capitalization.

Bank overdrafts line of credit. For companies with fluctuating income, a bank overdraft can provide quick, flexible cash flow but it can be like playing Russian roulette with your finances. The idea is simple: you dip into the overdraft in the leaner months, and come back out when the business picks up.

Most major banks charge interest only on the amount you overdraw, and many offer tailored packages for young businesses. For example, banks can provide overdrafts up to $500, free of set-up fees, for start-up firms if they are hungry for new business depositors. However rates of interest on bank overdrafts are usually charged above base rates, and in most cases the overdraft amount is repayable on demand.

Cash advances. Some companies such as Cashprior a subsidiary of Merchant Resources International are geared to offering money upfront, before debts and invoices have actually been paid.

Under the terms of the agreement, the financier purchases a fixed percentage of your future credit/debit card transactions at a discount, and then advances the cash into your bank account, usually within 10 working days. Repayments will be scheduled at a pre-agreed percentage of every transaction – usually between 10 and 20%.

With a cash advance, you can secure up to $100,000 without the burden of collateral or fixed monthly repayments. But you may have to meet a rigorous set of conditions; for example Business Cash Advance insists all clients must have been in business for at least a year, with a minimum monthly turnover of $3,500 and the ability to process credit and debit card transactions histories that average more than their loan service amount generally each month over some history that can be demonstrated. While there is no set rule this seems to be the norm.

Asset-based lending. An asset-based loan works the same way as a mortgage. You borrow money against an existing possession, and, if you can't meet your obligations, the asset is repossessed. Assets, which can be used as collateral, include property and premises, accounts receivable, inventory and equipment and even personal assets in many cases.

Although interest rates are often very punitive, asset-based finance can be extremely useful for a company desperate for cash, and/or a business backed by valuable property which has yet to make major profits – such as a hotels or restaurants. In this economy many individuals and small businesses have been forced to turn to Hard Money Lenders, especially with banks having gone missing in leading the revival of credit for individuals and companies that should be normally eligible for credit.

Factoring. The factoring process allows you to release the money tied up in unpaid invoices (account receivables), and removes much of the burden of debt management, but there is a risk for uncollected debts that could come back on the business getting the advance against their A/Rs. When you engage a factor, they will normally take control of your invoices and assume responsibility for processing them and collections. You will be able to draw funds as soon as the invoice has been approved in most cases – before the money actually comes in.

Factoring can speed up cash flow and free up the time spent chasing bad debts, but there are drawbacks and risks. A factor will impose a charge on each invoice, so your profit margins will be reduced, and it can be difficult to sever a contract with a factoring firm, because you have to compensate them for all outstanding invoices before you can formally part company. In addition, this can be an expensive overhead to cash starved businesses and eventually the lower margins could take a toll on the business.

Merchant Account Loans- A new trend that is different than traditional factoring but catching on quickly. Companies such as Paramount Merchant Funding and 2CPUSA are leading innovators in this concept.

Angel investors. If you manage to impress a business angel, they may provide investment in return for an equity stake. Most angels are seasoned entrepreneurs themselves, so they know what you're going through and they're likely to be patient.

Furthermore, the process of finding and enticing an angel is far less daunting than you might think. Companies can put you in touch with hundreds of angel investors, and provide advice to hone your pitch. If you can put together a tight pitch with realistic growth projections, and are prepared to give up a share of your business, this could be the route for you. A good starting point is Gust.com where they will allow you to search for the type of Angels interested in your business venture.

Crowd-funding. Crowdfunding is an extension of the highly mobile-networked folks that have similar interests in what I call cause related investments mainly. People come together on crowdfunding sites, to pool money towards a particular venture or idea and to feel good about putting small amounts of money at risk– it could be ten people putting in $500 each, or 3,000 people each giving $1. The advent of gaming and interactive role-playing has made crowdfunding something that to our young adults does not seem odd at all. CrowdfundingBank.com and

Microventures.com are examples of new innovations in this space.

Peer-to-peer loans. A peer-to-peer exchange sites, such as prosper.com will put you in touch with private lenders, and create a personal relationship between you and the lender – fostering trust and patience.

A number of companies are now well established in this space, and several offer generous terms.

Micro-loans. If you only need a very small amount of money, you should think about a micro loan, which is tailored to your circumstances and can be used alongside funding from other sources.

A number of companies in the USA and Europe offer micro loans; even one high school started a program sponsored by their students at Meadows School in Las Vegas, NV. These type programs offer small loans, with generous repayment terms ranging from one to five years.

Local Economic Development Community Schemes. A plethora of community development finance initiatives, exist today such as Local Economic Development Revolving Loan Funds, Local Seed Capital funds, Local Venture Capital Funds, community based EB5 Immigration funds for new business ventures, State economic development programs and even conduit financing structures, of course the banks do eventually participate in these type programs. There are numerous free resources to help with your business plan such as your local SCORE office and Small Business Development Center. These community based resources are in place to assist businesses that have found using the banking system unfavorable to their needs, especially to work through the reasons and create plausible mitigation for individuals, and businesses, denied credit by banks, lending companies, and other equity investor to create a responsible solution to such problems if possible.

Local Economic Development sources can help with everything from bridging loans and working capital to funds for property and equipment purchase, but their terms are usually aimed at smaller capital deals of $100K or less; you don't have to be a micro-business or a social enterprise, nor be based in a disadvantaged area to qualify for these programs, however there are special incentives for those businesses that do.

Family loans. If you want to keep things ultra-simple, a supportive family, with money to spare, can provide a fair, willing and reliable source of loan funding. Relatives and loved ones are more likely to trust you with their money than an outsider, and they will probably demand lower interest and fewer incentives than a commercial organization. The best way to approach a family loan is to show your willingness to collateralize their investment with real items if possible they will hold onto until you buy them back from you, sort of like your own internal pawn shop system. Example(s); I have a few here. You own your own Car, so provide them with the title signed over to them for 60% of the fair market value. You have the right to purchase the car back for whatever term above this per your security note, which can be the face amount of for some increment above that such as 70%, 80% or so on up to 100%. While this can be steep it is a quick source to patient funding. You must insure, maintain and provide for proper care of any items given to them in paper ownership transfer as your part of the deal. By offering to do this you look legitimate and they feel more secure about their loans. You can also use Boats, motorcycles, livestock, jewelry, computers, or anything the other party feels has a significant value. After all at our roots this was how all business was conducted in simpler times... it was a barter and exchange system. Perhaps they had it right after all.

Any finance model or provider should be researched thoroughly before you make any commitments, to ensure this is the best solution for your business. You will find more information on some of these finance options by visiting their websites. We would also recommend researching specific providers or funding platforms by checking references, better business bureaus and speaking to other businesses, which have had experience with the business service provider, is always essential.

Chapter 5:

Using Friends/Family/Investors

Given the dismal returns in the stock market in 2011 and not much potential to look for in 2012, people are increasingly shunning the stock market and looking for other places to put their money. Bringing in outside capital brings its own set of challenges, so make sure to manage expectations in the beginning and put agreement on paper, no matter how informal the relationship. Deciding on whether to raise investment or borrow money is the subject of another article, basically equity sales are good because they don't require any repayment (the hope is you will though), and most businesses don't turn a profit for a significant time period, which makes paying back loans extremely difficult. The downside to equity is that it is expensive when you consider selling a part of the company. If you are an established business and have ongoing financing needs, then loans make a lot more sense. Loans are easier to deal with when a company has a financial history to prove reliable repayment and an established company likely has more collateral to secure the loan. Note that most investors are probably not going to be interested in small, home based businesses but are looking for businesses that can quickly scale and can potentially make them a lot of money.

Friends and family typically need fewer assurances than investors because they are investing in you as much as the idea and are usually more patient if the business takes longer than expected to be profitable. Regardless of whether you are borrowing from family and friends instead of asking them to invest, maintain a very businesslike and impersonal relationship. Be aware of the old adage that friends and money sometimes don't mix, which is especially true in business and can strain relationships. Profits rarely come in as you projected and cash flow during the first few years can make it really difficult to pay back on a consistent schedule. To avoid putting strain on the relationship, don't over promise and draw up a formal agreement.

Outside of friends and family there are people in the community looking for investment possibilities. People such as doctors, dentists, accountants, attorneys and other high wealth individuals and business people that may either invest individually or join groups of other investors to make investments in small businesses. Typically investors look to invest in businesses within a certain industry that they know.

2012 is a great time to start a business and the rates are really attractive, no matter which route you take. Be sure to prepare a business plan and project the potential for success before getting money for your business.

Loved ones, friends, and friends-of-friends are the best place to start your search for capital. About three-quarters of start-up capital for the nation's small businesses is provided from family and friends or business owners themselves.

If you borrow from family or friends for your small business, only take money from people you know that can afford to lose it. If someone won't be able to feed their family and if your business goes under, don't take a dime from them. Also, only borrow from people who are relaxed about money and won't be butting into your business every day to see how "their" money is being spent. One of my favorite approaches to asking for funding from your friends and family consider signing over convertible debt instruments such as personal assets they know you cherish and will want to purchase back from them. It is a more personal version of bartering and pawn brokering only you can usually trust your friends and family members to allow you to purchase your items back once you have cash flow to do so. This was how the economy just a little over a hundred years ago was built for centuries. This method may make your friends and relatives feel more secure in their investment in you and also tend to valve off the harping on you for the repayment of their funds. Of course if you don't repay them with generous forgiveness of some oversight to timing they may either sell the item and/or just keep it. You have to be prepared for the worst case in this scenario, but at least you proved you had some valuable skin in the game and are taking the losses right along with others if the business fails.

An even better financing bet than friends is acquaintances. To find acquaintances that are looking for an investment, ask your accountant or attorney and network, network, network. People that know you and/or your business and can recommend it as an investment to their clients and friends. Also, tell colleagues and friends you are looking for an investor. If you talk about it to enough people, someone will eventually turn up hopefully.

Chapter 6:
Economic Development Revolving Loan Funds

In years leading up to 2008, the economic development industry was a leading provider of secondary and/or subordinated loans that could be used to create some additional risk reduction for small to medium businesses seeking capital. Since the meltdown of 2008 and the failure of banks to take on their responsibility to commence lending to small and medium businesses the economic development industry has been almost as abysmal in their own attention to the details of their prior leadership in small business lending. A case could be made that both banks and economic development organizations have been absent in leading their local economies out of the frozen wilderness of the post 2008 recession transition back to sustainable growth. It has been a failure to lead and invest in their core areas of responsibilities. Today many economic developers take the approach that the client has to come to them with a pre-packaged project and all the financing wrapped in a proverbial bow of opportunity.

A typical Economic Development revolving loan program would usually take a position of between twenty percent (20%) to forty percent (40%) of a project financing cost in a subordinated second lien position to the banks. This gave the banks a much lower risk relationship with their business clients. Normally these loans from the Community based revolving loan fund were easier to qualify for, based on job creation promises and investment into key equipment or facilities that would make the business more profitable and competitive, in theory thus giving them a better chance of staying in business and being a vibrant member of the local business economy. Economic Development lending generally is focused on job creation, economic diversification goals of the community leaders, investment into new or improving facilities in the local economy and/or expanding the products or services of the company creating a greater market share.

Yet, there are still a few resilient survivors in the small business-lending sector of community-based lenders in the economic development industry and finding them can worth the effort. The popularity and resurgence of organizations focused on finance is slowly rebuilding capacity in this sector. A comprehensive list of small community lenders can be found at organizations such as the Council of Community Finance Agencies and National Association of Development Organizations. Slowly community leaders are recognizing the need for them to recapitalize their local investment options and begin to invest in their own small to medium businesses as their key area of responsibility.

There is a fairly comprehensive list of economic development related business loan lenders at the Comprehensive directory of USA business loan funds by quasi-governmental agencies; http://www.businessloanfunds.com/

The first step is to approach your local economic development organization and asking them about whether they invest in local business projects and if so what criteria they may have for doing so. While the numbers of economic developers that actually may be competent at assisting in the development of financing of businesses has undoubtedly shrunk over the past decade and in many cases they have just depleted their local revolving loan funds and hung out the shingle... out of capital without mustering the recapitalization efforts in these tough economic times to rebuild this vital tool to local economic growth. There are still many that are still in business, some limping along and others doing rather well.

The popularity of the US Small Business Administration loan program as taken up much of this slack but not enough in my opinion. Their website is a treasure trove of information on applying for the various federally backed loan programs. www.sba.gov

Still if you are going to approach your local economic development organization for funding consideration and/or assistance in developing capitalization you need to have your business case and appeal to them for their support targeted on their stated priorities. This means you have to do your homework ahead of time and go in with a pitch that is simply too appealing for them to resist. It has been said that this is both an art and science so practice and experience in such dealings does matter. You may want to seek the expertise of an expert consultant in engaging your local financial opportunities rather than leave this to chance. Many folks shy away from this because the fees for most traditional consultants can make this seem fairly costly. It was for this reason that my own firm developed the performance-based model of consulting. Seeking out a performance based consultant or outcome oriented success fee driven consulting engagement can be a wise decision and fairly inexpensive to the entrepreneur and/or business owners.

Chapter 7:
"Using the Small Business Loan & Grant Programs of the US Government"

While much of my focus has been on non-traditional capital sources this does not mean that you should forgo investigating the use of what might be applicable lending or grant sources for your business idea or company. I am going to review what I consider to be the most productive of those programs in this chapter. Again, you may need to hire a professional like myself to best evaluate whether these sources make the best sense for you and your business. There relatively few truly legitimate government grants to traditional businesses unless they are negotiated as part of a business incentive program as I discuss in this book, but there is at least a few examples outlined in this chapter of both traditional loans and grants that might be of use to your business. This information was mostly taken directly from the various websites of each program and/or agency so that they are explained as the US government has decided is in the most definitive and descriptive marketing of these concepts. My intention is this chapter is simply to make you fully aware of their existence so you do not unknowingly overlook these as opportunities that might be applicable to your own business capitalization needs.

SBA 504

The CDC/504 loan program is a long-term financing tool, designed to encourage economic development within a community. The 504 Program accomplishes this by providing small businesses with long-term, fixed-rate financing to acquire major fixed assets for expansion or modernization.

A Certified Development Company (CDC) is a private, nonprofit corporation, which is set up to contribute to economic development within its community. CDCs work with SBA and private sector lenders to provide financing to small businesses, which accomplishes the goal of community economic development. Typically, a CDC/504 project includes:

- A loan secured from a private sector lender with a senior lien covering up to 50 percent of the project cost
- A loan secured from a CDC (backed by a 100 percent SBA-guaranteed debenture) with a junior lien covering up to 40 percent of the project cost
- A contribution from the borrower of at least 10 percent of the project cost (equity)

This type of setup means that 100% of the project cost is covered either by contribution of equity by the borrower, or the senior or junior lien.

SBA 7A

The 7(a) Loan Program is the SBA's primary program to help start-up and existing small businesses obtain financing when they might not be eligible for business loans through normal lending channels. The name comes from section 7(a) of the Small Business Act, which authorizes the SBA to provide business loans to American small businesses. The SBA itself does not make loans, but rather guarantees a portion of loans made and administered by commercial lending institutions.

7(a) loans are the most basic and most commonly used type of loans. They are also the most flexible, since financing can be guaranteed for a variety of general business purposes, including working capital, machinery and equipment, furniture and fixtures, land and building (including purchase, renovation and new construction), leasehold improvements, and debt refinancing (under special conditions). Loan maturity is up to 10 years for working capital and generally up to 25 years for fixed assets.

Most American banks participate in the program, as do some non-bank lenders, which can expand the availability of loans. Participating lenders agree to structure loans according to the SBA's requirements, and apply and receive a guaranty from the SBA on a portion of this loan. The SBA does not fully guarantee 7(a) loans—the lender and the SBA share the risk that a borrower will not be able to repay the loan in full. The guaranty is against payment default; it does not cover imprudent decisions by the lender or misrepresentation by the borrower.

SBA Microloan Program:

The Microloan Program provides small, short-term loans to small business concerns and certain types of not-for-profit child-care centers. The SBA makes funds available to specially designated intermediary lenders, which are nonprofit community-based organizations with experience in lending as well as management and technical assistance. These intermediaries make loans to eligible borrowers. The maximum loan amount is $50,000, but the average microloan is about $13,000.

Microloans may be used for the following purposes:

- Working capital
- The purchase of inventory or supplies
- The purchase of furniture or fixtures
- The purchase of machinery or equipment.

Proceeds from a microloan cannot be used to pay existing debts or to purchase real estate.

USDA Rural Business & Industry (B&I) Loan Program

The purpose of the B&I Guaranteed Loan Program is to improve, develop, or finance business, industry, and employment and improve the economic and environmental climate in rural communities. This purpose is achieved by bolstering the existing private credit structure through the guarantee of quality loans, which will provide lasting community benefits. It is not intended that the guarantee authority will be used for marginal or substandard loans or for relief of lenders having such loans.

Who May Borrow?

A borrower may be a cooperative organization, corporation, partnership, or other legal entity organized and operated on a profit or nonprofit basis; an Indian tribe on a Federal or State reservation or other Federally recognized tribal group; a public body; or an individual. A borrower must be engaged in or proposing to engage in a business that will:

- Provide employment;
- Improve the economic or environmental climate;
- Promote the conservation, development, and use of water for aquaculture; or
- Reduce reliance on nonrenewable energy resources by encouraging the development and construction of solar energy systems and other renewable energy systems.

Individual borrowers must be citizens of the United States (U.S.) or reside in the U.S. after being legally admitted for permanent residence. Corporations or other nonpublic body organization-type borrowers must be at least 51 percent owned by persons who are either citizens of the U.S. or reside in the U.S. after being legally admitted for permanent residence. B&I loans are normally available in rural areas, which include all areas other than cities or towns of more than 50,000 people and the contiguous and adjacent urbanized area of such cities or towns.

How May the Funds be Used?

Loan purposes must be consistent with the general purpose contained in the regulation. They include but are not limited to the following:

- Business and industrial acquisitions when the loan will keep the business from closing, prevent the loss of employment opportunities, or provide expanded job opportunities.
- Business conversion, enlargement, repair, modernization, or development.
- Purchase and development of land, easements, rights-of-way, buildings, or facilities.
- Purchase of equipment, leasehold improvements, machinery, supplies, or inventory.

What is the percentage of Guarantee?

The percentage of guarantee, up to the maximum allowed, is a matter of negotiation between the lender and the Agency. The maximum percentage of guarantee is 80 percent for loans of $5 million or less, 70 percent for loans between $5 and $10 million, and 60 percent for loans exceeding $10 million.

What are the Loan Amounts?

The total amount of Agency loans to one borrower must not exceed $10 million. The Administrator may, at the Administrator discretion, grant an exception to the $10 million limit for loans of $25 million under certain circumstances. The Secretary may approve guaranteed loans in excess of $25 million, up to $40 million, for rural cooperative organizations that process value-added agricultural commodities.

What are the Loan Terms?

The maximum repayment for loans on real estate will not exceed 30 years; machinery and equipment repayment will not exceed the useful life of the machinery and equipment purchased with loan funds or 15 years, whichever is less; and working capital repayment will not exceed 7 years.

What are the Interest Rates?

The interest rate for the guaranteed loan will be negotiated between the lender and the applicant and may be either fixed or variable as long as it is a legal rate. Interest rates are subject to Agency review and approval. The variable interest rate may be adjusted at different intervals during the term of the loan, but the adjustments may not be more often than quarterly.

Is Collateral Required?

Yes. Collateral must have documented value sufficient to protect the interest of the lender and the Agency. The discounted collateral value will normally be at least equal to the loan amount. Lenders will discount collateral consistent with sound loan-to-value policy.

Is there an Annual Renewal Fee?

The annual renewal fee is paid once a year and is required to maintain the enforceability of the guarantee as to the lender.

The rate of the annual renewal fee (a specified percentage) is established by Rural Development in an annual notice published in the Federal Register, multiplied by the outstanding principal loan balance as of December 31 of each year, multiplied by the percent of guarantee. The rate is the rate in effect at the time the loan is obligated, and will remain in effect for the life of the loan.

Annual renewal fees are due on January 31. Payments not received by April 1 are considered delinquent and, at the Agency discretion, may result in cancellation of the guarantee to the lender. Holdersrights will continue in effect as specified in the Loan Note Guarantee and Assignment Guarantee Agreement. Any delinquent annual renewal fees will bear interest at the note rate and will be deducted from any loss payment due the lender. For loans where the Loan Note Guarantee is issued between October 1 and December 31, the first annual renewal fee payment will be due January 31 of the second year following the date the Loan Note Guarantee was issued.

Where Should Applications be Filed?

Complete applications should be sent to the USDA Rural Development State Office for the project location. A list of offices and additional information can be obtained at http://www.rurdev.usda.gov/recd_map.html.

SBIOR

The SBIR Program

The Small Business Innovation Research (SBIR) program is a highly competitive program that encourages domestic small businesses to engage in Federal Research/Research and Development (R/R&D) that has the potential for commercialization. Through a competitive awards-based program, SBIR enables small businesses to explore their technological potential and provides the incentive to profit from its commercialization. By including qualified small businesses in the nation's R&D arena, high-tech innovation is stimulated and the United States gains entrepreneurial spirit as it meets its specific research and development needs.

SBIR Mission and Program Goals

The mission of the SBIR program is to support scientific excellence and technological innovation through the investment of Federal research funds in critical American priorities to build a strong national economy.

The program's goals are four-fold:

- Stimulate technological innovation
- Meet Federal research and development needs.
- Foster and encourage participation in innovation and entrepreneurship by socially and economically disadvantaged persons.
- Increase private-sector commercialization of innovations derived from Federal research and development funding.

SBIR-Participating Agencies

Each year, Federal agencies with extramural research and development (R&D) budgets that exceed $100 million are required to allocate 2.5 percent of their R&D budget to these programs. Currently, eleven Federal agencies participate in the program:

- Department of Agriculture
- **Department of Commerce** - National Institute of Standards and Technology
- **Department of Commerce** - National Oceanic and Atmospheric Administration
- Department of Defense
- Department of Education
- Department of Energy
- Department of Health and Human Services
- Department of Homeland Security
- Department of Transportation
- Environmental Protection Agency
- National Aeronautics and Space Administration
- National Science Foundation

Each agency administers its own individual program within guidelines established by Congress. These agencies designate R&D topics in their solicitations and accept proposals from small businesses. Awards are made on a competitive basis after proposal evaluation.

Three-Phase Program

The SBIR Program is structured in three phases:

Phase I. The objective of Phase I is to establish the technical merit, feasibility, and commercial potential of the proposed R/R&D efforts and to determine the quality of performance of the small business awardee organization prior to providing further Federal support in Phase II. SBIR Phase I awards normally do not exceed $150,000 total costs for 6 months.

Phase II. The objective of Phase II is to continue the R/R&D efforts initiated in Phase I. Funding is based on the results achieved in Phase I and the scientific and technical merit and commercial potential of the project proposed in Phase II. Only Phase I awardees are eligible for a Phase II award. SBIR Phase II awards normally do not exceed $1,000,000 total costs for 2 years.

Phase III. The objective of Phase III, where appropriate, is for the small business to pursue commercialization objectives resulting from the Phase I/II R/R&D activities. The SBIR program does not fund Phase III. Some Federal agencies, Phase III may involve follow-on non-SBIR funded R&D or production contracts for products, processes or services intended for use by the U.S. Government.

SBIR Program Eligibility

Only United States small businesses are eligible to participate in the SBIR program. Business must meet *all* of the following criteria at the time of Phase I and II awards:

- Organized for profit, with a place of business located in the United States;
- At least 51 percent owned and controlled by one or more individuals who are citizens of, or permanent resident aliens in, the United States, or
- At least 51 percent owned and controlled by another for-profit business concern that is at least 51% owned and controlled by one or more individuals who are citizens of, or permanent resident aliens in, the United States; and;
- No more than 500 employees, including affiliates.

SBIR differs from STTR in two important aspects:

- The principal investigator must have primary employment with the SBC (unless a waiver is granted by the agency).

- SBIR encourages but does not require the SBC to partner with a research institution.

Congressional History

The SBIR program was established under the Small Business Innovation Development Act of 1982 (P.L. 97-219) with the purpose of strengthening the role of innovative small business concerns in federally funded research and development (R&D). Through FY2009, over 112,500 awards have been made totaling more than $26.9 billion.

In December 2000, Congress passed the Small Business Research and Development Enhancement Act (P.L. 102-564), reauthorizing the SBIR program until September 30, 2000. The program was reauthorized until September 30, 2008 by the Small Business Reauthorization Act of 2000 (P.L. 106-554). Subsequently, Congress passed numerous extensions, the most recent of which extends the SBIR program through 2017.

Competitive Opportunity for Small Business

SBIR targets the entrepreneurial sector because that is where most innovation and innovators thrive. However, the risk and expense of conducting serious R&D efforts are often beyond the means of many small businesses. By reserving a specific percentage of federal R&D funds for small businesses, SBIR protects the small business and enables it to compete on the same level as larger businesses. SBIR funds the critical startup and development stages and it encourages the commercialization of the technology, product, or service, which, in turn, stimulates the U.S. economy. Since its enactment in 1982, the SBIR program has helped thousands of small businesses to compete for federal R&D awards. Their contributions have enhanced the nation's defense, protected our environment, advanced health care, and improved our ability to manage information and manipulate data.

SBA Role

The US Small Business Administration serves as the coordinating agency for the SBIR program. It directs the agencies' implementation of SBIR, reviews their progress, and reports annually to Congress on its operation. SBA is also the information link to SBIR program.

For more information on the SBIR Program, please contact:

US Small Business Administration Office of Technology 409 Third Street, SW Washington, DC 20416 (202) 205-6450
http://www.sbir.gov/about/about-sbir

Federally Sponsored Venture Capital Programs:

Venture capital is a type of equity financing that addresses the funding needs of entrepreneurial companies that for reasons of size, assets, and stage of development cannot seek capital from more traditional sources, such as public markets and banks. Venture capital investments are generally made as cash in exchange for shares and an active role in the invested company.

- The New Markets Venture Capital Companies The New Markets Venture Capital (NMVC) program seeks to stimulate economic development in Low Income (LI) areas. Through public-private partnerships between the SBA and newly formed NMVC Companies (NMVCCs) and existing Specializedhttp://www.sba.gov/content/new-markets-venture-capital-companies

All SBIC Licensees by State The Small Business Investment Company (SBIC) Program provides venture capital to small businesses. Although SBICs are licensed and regulated by SBA, they are private, profit-seeking investment companies. This directory will provide you with access to the most appropriate SBIC in your area. http://www.sba.gov/content/all-sbic-licensees-states

Typical Checklist for Applying for Federally Backed Loans & Grants

SBA is not the only source for small-business loans. State and local economic-development agencies – and numerous nonprofit organizations – provide low-interest loans to small business owners who may not qualify for traditional commercial loans.

When it comes to applying for these loans, the good news is that most of these other lenders require the same kinds of information. Of course, each loan program has specific forms you need to fill out. But for the most part, you'll need to submit the same types of documentation. So it's a good idea to gather what you'll need before you even start the application process.

Here are the typical items required for any small business loan application:

Loan Application Form

Forms vary by program and lending institution, but they all ask for the same information. You should be prepared to answer the following questions. It's a good idea to have this information prepared before you fill out the application:

- Why are you applying for this loan?
- How will the loan proceeds be used?
- What assets need to be purchased, and who are your suppliers?
- What other business debt do you have, and who are your creditors?
- Who are the members of your management team?

- Personal Background

Either as part of the loan application or as a separate document, you will likely need to provide some personal background information, including previous addresses, names used, criminal record, educational background, etc.

Resumes

Some lenders require evidence of management or business experience, particularly for loans that can be used to start a new business.

Business Plan

All loan programs require a sound business plan to be submitted with the loan application. The business plan should include a complete set of projected financial statements, including profit and loss, cash flow and balance sheet.

Here are some resources for preparing your business plan:

- Essential Elements of Writing a Good Business Plan
- Templates for Writing a Business Plan
- Personal Credit Report

Your lender will obtain your personal credit report as part of the application process. However, you should obtain a credit report from all three major consumer credit rating agencies before submitting a loan application to the lender. Inaccuracies and blemishes on your credit report can hurt your chances of getting a loan approved. It's critical you try to clear these up before beginning the application process.

Business Credit Report

If you are already in business, you should be prepared to submit a credit report for your business. As with the personal credit report, it is important to review your business' credit report before beginning the application process.

Income Tax Returns

Most loan programs require applicants to submit personal and business income tax returns for the previous three years.

Financial Statements

Many loan programs require owners with more than a 20 percent stake in your business to submit signed personal financial statements.

You may also be required to provide projected financial statements either as part of, or separate from your business plan. It is a good idea to have these prepared and ready in case a program for which you are applying requires these documents to be submitted individual.

The following forms may be used to prepare your projected financial statements:

- Balance Sheet
- Income Statement
- Cash Flow
- Bank Statements

Many loan programs require one year of personal and business bank statements to be submitted as part of a loan package.

Accounts Receivable and Accounts Payable

Most loan programs require details of a business's most current financial position. Before you begin the loan application process, make sure you have accounts receivable and accounts payable.

Collateral

Collateral requirements vary greatly. Some loan programs do not require collateral. Loans involving higher risk factors for default require substantial collateral. Strong business plans and financial statements can help you avoid putting up collateral. In any case, it is a good idea to prepare a collateral document that describes cost/value of personal or business property that will be used to secure a loan.

Legal Documents

Depending on a loan's specific requirements, your lender may require you to submit one or more legal documents. Make sure you have the following items in order, if applicable:

- Business licenses and registrations required for you to conduct business
- Articles of Incorporation
- Copies of contracts you have with any third parties
- Franchise agreements
- Commercial leases
- Organizing your documents

Keeping good records is essential for running a successful business, but even more critical when applying for a loan. Make sure required documents are orderly and accurate. Your lender and the organization guaranteeing the loan will verify all information you provide. False or misleading information will result in your loan being denied. Finally, make sure you keep personal copies of all loan packages.

Chapter 8:
New Market Tax Credit Programs

The creation of the NMTC program has been one of a host of conundrums for the financing industry. It has struggled to gain understanding and acceptance amongst the small business lending industry both within traditional banks and the economic development industry. It may be linked to the difficulty of comprehensive understanding of how to use this tool. It is in my own opinion the brain fart of some very seriously smart Washington consultants, but it was too heady for most of the laypeople that had to implement it. None-the-less, Washington in their normal style has failed to recognize this difficulty and has refused to make the program more easily adapted to the local economic development community lending needs. This has resulted in many unused allocations going without borrowers, this in a time when the dust bowl of small business needs could lead a sip of water from the credit markets. The following is a good overview of how this cumbersome program works.

1. The federal government authorizes the tax credits.

- The amount of annual credit authority (or allocation authority) is authorized by Congress.
- The Community Development Financial Institutions Fund (CDFI Fund) under the Department of the Treasury reviews applications and awards allocation authority to qualified Community Development Entities (CDEs) through a competitive process.

2. Each of the CDE's then determine what projects get funded.

- CDEs can receive investments called Qualified Equity Investments (QEI) from investors up to the amount of the allocation authority that the CDE has from the CDFI Fund.

- CDEs use the QEI dollars received from investors to make a loan or equity investment in a project or business called a Qualified Active Low-Income Community Business (QALICB). The projects and financing must be consistent with the way the CDE described their business plan in their application to CDFI for consideration. The financing proceeds can be used for a variety of purposes, and are often used to construct or rehabilitate real estate projects that are over loaned or fall short in reaching the traditional loan to value ratios required by traditional lenders

3. Developers and business owners can get flexible financing if they qualify for the NMTC.

- CDEs are required to offer financing that has terms that are non-traditional or more flexible than conventional financing thus the blended loan cost to the business can achieve some cost savings in capital expense by using this approach.
- Borrowers benefit from below market interest rates and underwriting terms that they could not receive from conventional financing.
- Many CDEs will only fund transactions that would not have been done "but for" the NMTC, in other words, a project either could not qualify for any conventional financing, or could not qualify for enough to cover the entire cost of the project without the subsidy created by NMTC. This was the original intent in my mind of the program.

4. Low income communities benefit from investments.

- NMTC projects are selected by CDEs in part based on the community impact that will be achieved. This is linked to census tracts and what are referred to in many cases as Difficult to Development Areas (DDAs).

- Communities benefit from newly created construction and permanent jobs, improved access to goods and services including both retail and human services, and new recreation and entertainment options.
- Increased visibility and consumer traffic in previously underserved markets can encourage future development and creates the intended windfall that Congress has hoped for by creating this program.

5. Investors get a 39% tax credit over a seven-year period.
- The tax credit is based on the amount of the QEI that is made into the CDE; investors receive 5% per year in the first three years and 6% per year in the final four years. Some high wealth individuals with a taxable income need for some reduction in their tax bills could find this program attractive.

The QEI can be made up of an equity investment from the tax credit investor plus "leverage loans" from banks, affiliates of the QALICB or other third parties such as cities, state agencies or other funding sources.

A good source of over-all information about this non-traditional program is available at the New Markets Tax Credits Coalition http://nmtccoalition.org/

Chapter 9:
EB5 Immigration Investment Program

The EB-5 Visa Allows Foreigners to Live Permanently in the United States if they invest in qualified projects and/or businesses.

For foreign investors seeking the freedom and flexibility to live and work in the United States, the EB-5 Visa Program provides an excellent opportunity to obtain their Green Cards.

A Green Card provides Permanent Residency for the applicant, his or her spouse and any offspring under the age of 21. The EB5 investment visa route to a green card avoids the usual requirement of having family connections, securing a job or running an actively traded business - making it a viable route to retirement.

Section 610 of Public Law 102-395 created the Immigrant Investor Pilot Program on October 6, 1992. This was in accordance to a Congressional mandate aimed at stimulating economic activity and job growth, while allowing eligible aliens the opportunity to become lawful permanent residents.

This "Pilot Program" required only $500,000 of investment in exchange for permanent resident status. An economic unit defined as regional centers could only receive the investment. Today the majority is now required to invest one million in order to qualify. Just as most economic development oriented financing programs the EB5 is targeted at specific objectives and one of them is of course job creation. The designation varies but the target employment areas (TEA) generally have needs that are 150% greater than the USA average unemployment averages. Investor projects have to create at least 10 US jobs for their investment.

A good resource to utilize in finding out if your area has a Regional Center is the following organization, the Association to Invest in the USA their website is https://iiusa.org/

72

Chapter 10:
Types of Bonds for Small to Medium businesses

There are a number of ways to use the bond markets to assist small to medium size business that are often overlooked. For now I am going to focus on the most common and available bond tools. They are the Industrial Revenue Bond (IRB) programs, Private Activity Bonds and Municipal Utility District Bonds, Special Improvement district bonds, and municipal and/or state allocated bond pools aimed at economic development objectives. One such program is the STAR bond program. Each state will have a different approach to these types of bonds and some states do not use all of these approaches. Again being informed enough to ask your economic development officials about these programs is a great start to your quest for capitalization of your business needs.

Most states and many local governments offer industrial revenue bonds (IRB) as a way to encourage relocations and expansions of companies that provide jobs and expand economic opportunities for residents and the community. IRBs are an incentive to encourage a company to invest in local economy.

What is an IRB? An Industrial Revenue Bond, or IRB, is a loan to a company to build or buy a facility or buy land and/or equipment. IRBs are one of the ways local governments and states can encourage relocation and expansion and retention of investments in their local economies.

How do they work? Typically the city or economic development conduit jurisdictional authority issues the bonds but is not making the loan. The investor buying the bond makes the loan. The company must find its own bond purchaser. It can also buy its own IRBs. The government conduit authority technically owns title to the facility built with IRBs and leases it to the company for up to 20 years. At the end of the term, title is transferred to the company.

Do IRBs affect the credit ratings of the jurisdictional authority or conduit financial organization? No. Since the conduit organization is not responsible for the loan, the IRB does not have an impact on their credit rating.

Can a small business use an IRB? Because of financing costs, IRBs are typically used for larger capital projects. They are generally not recommended for projects less than $2 million.

What are the steps to apply for an IRB?

1. After a company identifies a site, its representatives meet with the appropriate jurisdictional authority responsible for this form of conduit financing to get support and identify any potential concerns.

2. The company identifies a purchaser for the bonds this can be a host of different sources including local banks. There are also in most states IRB packagers and analysts that can place these for the business owner.

3. The company prepares a project description and calculates potential employment and submits an application, which includes the company's financial information, to the Conduit Jurisdictional Authority.

4. The Conduit Authority will normally prepare a staff analysis for review by their board of directors.

5. Their board of directors usually will hold a public hearing and makes a recommendation to either issue the IRBs or not.

6. After passage of the ordinance or allocation, the attorneys will prepare closing documents covering the transaction and send them to the bond purchasers escrow agents.

8. At closing the bond purchaser buys the bonds.

Private Activity bonds

A tax-exempt municipal bond in which a local government entity is seeking to raise money for a private company. A municipality issues a private activity bond when it wishes to attract and/or retain a business and the jobs it brings to the area, especially when the business may be otherwise unable to obtain financing for the project. This could be used to expand a business that has a unique market and is not easily defined by traditional lenders for comparative risk analysis. The municipality issuing the bond must be able to prove that a public benefit derives from the private activity bond in order to qualify for tax-exempt status. Private activity bonds generally are not guaranteed by the revenue of the municipality.

A very good explanation of the uses and restrictions and permissible funding opportunities for Private Activity Bonds is at the legal firm Smith Gambrell and Russell's website, http://www.sgrlaw.com/resources/briefings/bond_practice/456/

Another very interesting tool for financing business projects is the STAR Bond program, or Sales Tax Advance Revenue bonds. There are currently only a few states with this tool authorized currently and the leader is Kansas, which was the early adopter. Kansas has been followed by Nevada, Missouri and now Illinois is also looking at approval. In the near future states and communities starved to create highly visible destination tourism and retail oriented expenditures will be eyeing this tool like a prize. It probably won't be long until the major players such as Texas, Virginia, the Carolinas and Florida will more than likely follow suit.

A STAR bond calculates the sales tax revenue that will be created by a project and captures these sales into a district that catches all the sales tax proceeds and then applies some portion of those revenues to repay the bondholders. There have been some very large and innovative projects such as the Legends in Kansas City Area financed using this approach.

Special Improvement Districts a widely used economic development infrastructure tool and/or Municipal Utility Districts (MUDs) in Texas are special designed zones around targeted improvements within a specific location that creates the necessary wet, dry and other site improvements to enhance the ability for real estate development to be created. Then the zone or district places a tax or lien on all property holders or special assessment paid by each of them annually until the bonds are repaid.

Tax Increment Financing Bonds- These TIF bonds are used within areas called TIF districts normally. These TIF districts are zones around real estate that pools the real estate taxes or a portion of them for making targeted investments into businesses, infrastructure and other improvements to the real estate district that will enhance the attractiveness of the area, remove blight and thus create opportunities for redevelopment, mitigate other growth barriers or stimulate further investment into the district that will create jobs. Generally these TIF proceeds are what we refer to as "Pay as You Go," meaning the property owner just gets their taxes paid rebated each year towards a specific identified capital use or Issued debt against the future property taxes, which is more risky if the business fails and does not repay the TIF funds. TIF bonds usually are used to aggregate a number of capital uses for a larger number of businesses as a pooled credit tool. Most states with the exception of Arizona have TIF legislation of some form. The use of TIFs is getting more and more difficult as cities and counties face rising budget concerns and risks of shrinking revenue sources to meet their financial obligations that are outstanding.

One way around this is to offer to freeze the current real estate taxes and then ask for abatement on the taxes that would be applicable to the proposed improvements the business is making. This will count as equity contribution in your gross over-all project debt to equity ratio in most cases. It also reduces the operating costs of the business for the time period the TIF abatement is authorized by the appropriate jurisdictional authority. A normal TIF time period does not typically exceed ten years. Many TIFs also use a scaled approach abating 100% the first year after the improvement and then decreasing the abatement in 10% increments until it become fully utilized by the end of year ten (10).

Chapter 11:
Typical Public Sector Venture Fund Questions for a Business Application for Funding Consideration:

If you are considering the pursuit of venture capital and/or even initial seed capital or you believe you have what it takes to approach an Angel investor or Angel Investment group. You had better do your homework ahead of time. The following is a good guideline to understanding the types of basic information you should be prepared to provide for such meetings and proposal considerations. Of course in my opinion unless you have the capability for extraordinaire growth and high profitability this route would be difficult for most businesses and entrepreneurs, but not impossible. There have many examples of great successes. Please review the following do your own self-assessment to see how your business and/or business idea might stack up.

There are some good sources for information on Venture capital available at the following organizations;

The International Venture Capital Institute (IVCI)
PO Box 1333
Stamford, CT 06904
203-323-3143

Association of Venture Capital Clubs
265 East 100 South, Suite 300
PO Box 3358
Salt Lake City, UT 84111
801-364-1100

There are billions of dollars of venture capital available to businesses in all kinds of industries at a variety of stages of development. Currently, venture funds are in good positions to make investments, because the public market has given us the opportunity to sell holdings and increase our liquidity.

Most firms have millions of dollars to invest and provide money in sums ranging from $250,000 to $10 million or more. Most venture capitalists have set limits, minimums, and maximums they are willing to invest, and some specialize in certain regions of the country or industry. Other firms invest in any U.S. firm. Biotechnology and high technology are the most popular types of firms for venture capitalists, but service companies and other firms do receive venture money. Retail and consumer companies are of interest only if they have high expansion potential. Look through a list of venture firms for their geographic or industry specialization before making your contact list.

In general, the following characteristics are what venture firms are looking for:

- **Extraordinary growth potential:** The industry you are in or are entering must be able to support exponential growth. Venture-funded companies are expected to be able to grow to $50 to $100 million in less than ten years.
- **Management talent:** Venture capitalists must be convinced that you and the others in your company are capable of building a multi-million dollar business. You will probably need previous experience building and managing growth in the past or the ability to hire top people.
- **Proprietary products or services:** Patents, copyrights, trademarks, and other rights to a product or service will give you a great advantage in your pursuit of venture capital. Venture capitalists are looking for companies with an advantage over existing or potential competitors.

If you are looking for venture capital you also need to be on the lookout for scams they are very prevalent. I would highly warn you to avoid like the plague any request to give "upfront fees or deposits" to a firm that promises it will give you venture capital. There simply are no real guarantees on funding until you get a term sheet from an investor and/or financial institution. Disreputable people posing as venture capitalists, angels and high wealth individuals have bilked thousands of people out of thousands of dollars over the years by asking for "good faith" deposits. The excuses they use to collect these funds are lawyers fees, accounting reviews, travel expenses, research fees, phone call expenses, and document review fees.

TYPICAL VENTURE CAPITAL APPLICATION INFORMATION – QUALIFYING A BUSINESS for CONSIDERATION

1. The principal business operations of the business are located in the state governing the use of the funds.

    Please confirm that the operations of the qualifying business are located in the state providing the funding. Also, if the address of the qualifying business is different than the address noted on page 1 of the application, please list the address here.

2. The business has been in operation for three years or less at the date of the investment for which a credit is claimed for investments made prior to July 1, 2005, or the business has been in operation for six years or less at the date of the investment for which is credit is claimed for investments made on or after July 1, 2005.

    Please indicate the date when the operations of the qualifying business started and what state or domicile the corporation is registered in and if applicable is the company registered to do business in the state providing the funding.

3. The business has an owner who has successfully completed either an entrepreneurial venture development curriculum (such as programs developed by a Entrepreneurial Center,

SCORE or SBDC, or a holistic training program recognized by the State Government providing the funds); three years of relevant business experience; a four-year college degree in business management, business administration or a related field; or other training and experience is also preferred but not necessarily mandatory.

Please provide a signed statement from the owner stating which of the above criteria has been met.

4. The business is not engaged primarily in retail sales, real estate, or the provision of health care or other professional services in most cases there are some exceptions. "Professional services" include, but are not limited to, services provided by professions listed in your State Code Section that defines such and each state defines this differently.

Please state the product or service provided by the qualifying business.

5. The business must not have a net worth that exceeds usually $2 million to $3 million at the date of the investment for which the credit is claimed for investments made prior to a statutory requirement date, or the business must not have a net worth that exceeds $10 million at the date of the investment for which a credit is claimed for investments made on or after the statutory date.

Please state the net worth of the business.

6. The business shall have secured, within 24 months following the first date on which equity investments qualifying for tax credits have been made, total equity or near equity equal to usually some minimum amount starting at approximately $250,000. In many cases.

Please set forth the amount of secured investments that have been made to date.

7. Please provide a signed statement from an officer, director, manager, member or general partner of the business that contains: 1) a description of the general nature of the business, 2) the location of the business operations, 3) the date the business was formed, 4) the date the business commenced operations, and 5) a certificate of existence of a business plan which details the business' growth strategy, management team, production/management plan, marketing plan, financial plan and other standard elements of a business plan.

8. Please provide a balance sheet certified by the chief executive officer and chief financial officer of the business reflecting the business' assets, liabilities and owners' equity as of the close of the most recent month or quarter. You will need to become proficient in the language of finance and representing such business case facts to quasi-governmental bodies and/or governmental bodies with jurisdictional authority over the use of any such funds.

9. Please provide a signed statement from an officer, director, manager, member or general partner of the business that contains: 1) the names, addresses, shares or equity interests issued, consideration paid for the shares or equity interests, and the amount of tax credits of all shareholders or equity-holders who may initially qualify for the tax credits, and the earliest year in which the credits may be redeemed, and 2) a commitment by the business to amend its statement as may be necessary to reflect new equity interests or transfers in equity.

10. Please provide the uses of cash for the funds and any specific market analysis conducted that verifies the validity of the business concept and proposed use of these funds. Including additional term sheets from additional investors or

investment banking firms that will continue to raise additional debt or equity funding on behalf of the company.

Chapter 12:

The Conclusion for Possible Next Steps
Running the Gauntlet for Capitalization and getting Funding here are the Tasks Simplified:

Searching for capital is a daunting task these days with the credit markets frozen and banks acting like well greedy bankers and holding onto the necessary cash for small to medium businesses to expand, which in turn would instill faith in consumers through new jobs and investments they could see and feel being created in their own local economies. Market behavior is really linked to human behavior and our own human perceptions of the realities we perceive around us. Seeking capital has to play to these same tendencies. No longer are there many single source solutions for raising risk capital, borrowing leveraged debt or increasing working capital for expansion and growth.

The Art of the Deal Structure Today

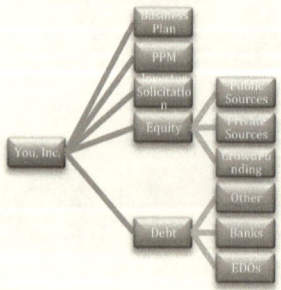

In order to raise monies today the approach to capital has to be broad but it has to have a very focused and tight story (business plan and business case) and a significant sophistication for approaching each sources with an investor solicitation tied to a private placement memorandum that meets state rules on non-qualified capital solicitation.

HERE ARE SOME EXAMPLES OF SOURCES OF FUNDING FOR USE IN CAPITALIZATION with Local Governments, that I have a great deal of knowledge in representing for my clients:

1. Land Grants, site improvements shovel ready, site infrastructure grants, environmental and soils inspections and fast track permitting and waiving impact fees and other local ordinance required permits for new development.

2. Community based revolving loan, seed capital, angel investor matching, venture capital funding, in-kind business services, bank and other investor coaching, as well as assisting in the business plan and business case for investment proposal development.

3. Grants and/or forgivable or low interest loans to perform the assembly of the entire due diligence package required to prove the business feasibility, market study, business case for investors, legal and financial incentives development and site selection for the business. This is by far what I consider to be the best way to secure funding as the partnership is essentially reverse engineering successful launch of a business, rather than the old shoot at everything approach of economic development. Of course if you can't convince your local community to believe in themselves and the

need for the product and/or service, I doubt the market will see the value much easier. This does not mean No is final, it just means Maybe and you haven't convinced them yet as to how to say YES.

4. Tax Abatement, Tax Increment Financing, and Tax deferred operating costs are very useful for existing businesses that could then use the internal reduction in costs to expand their business and hit their investors required IRR or ROI dividend expectations for profitability.

5. Special Government backed conduit financing utilizing existing programs and/or special legislation for these purposes. Again, this approach is generally aimed at small to medium high growth and high impact companies that already exist within a community and/or are seeking to expand their business to another state to grow their business.

Example Sources of Funds	$USD/Avg %
Angels (Investor Agreement) convertible Debt most likely	25%
Friends & Family (PPM) Equity	10%
Public Capital Sale (OTC) Equity	N/A
Crowd Funding (equity-PPM)	10%
Economic Development Sources	60%
Total	100%

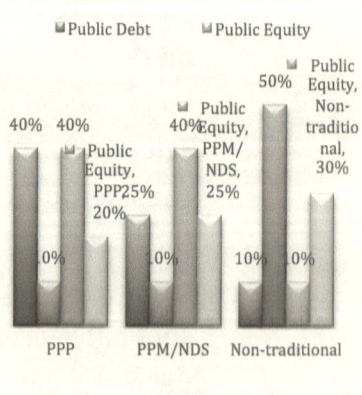

Public Private Partnerships (P3's)

Getting the right structure to your business case is essential. There are three very popular structures I recommend considering each with a different but similar approach to your overall capitalization strategy needs. The first is the Public-Private Partnership where the public sector desires to work with you in order to diversify their local economy and as such takes a larger share of risk in this effort to see your business through to fruition. This approach works best for companies that have been in business for more than 3 years and are typically profitable and just expanding their business operations. This is tied to job creation, business tax base in the future, and current and future direct and indirect as well as induced economic impact. The Urban Land Institute is a good resource for more information on this concept.

http://www.uli.org/ResearchAndPublications/Reports/~/media/Documents/ResearchAndPublications/Reports/TenPrinciples/TP_Partnerships.ashx

Private Placement Memorandum & Negotiated Debt Placement:

These type programs are heavily used for new ventures where the product is highly desired but the company is either brand new or outgrowing traditional banking fundamental lending requirements or perceived to be too new and risky for traditional lenders. This is the domain of the entrepreneurs. In order to raise monies that have a legal stake in your business entity you must have a legal way to ask folks for money and even then you are limited to the number depending on the type entity you choose and investment savvy and net worth of those that buy the stock. Each state is different and the state you choose to incorporate or domicile within is also a major consideration for shareholder protection and corporate protection of operating rights. I recommend you use a private placement memorandum and have your CPA/Attorney update the form for your own uses and your state requirements. You can get a whole host of forms fairly inexpensively at Growthink.com

Then you have to either decide to use many various offering and pitch forms to get attention to your business... this can be crowd funding, venture capital, seed capital, angels and even purchasing a delisted OTC (over the counter stock) and having it repositioned as your own company for your purposes. This has a very huge brand appeal when coupled with the community capital approach and crowd funding approach... but in my opinion it still requires a savvy lead angel investor and/or entrepreneur to be the expert pitchman or woman on the face of the company promotion for seeking capital. I am in no way endorsing any of these firms. One firm that states that they offer public stock exchange access for small companies to potentially go public is Tiber Creek Corporation. http://www.tcc5.com/

Non-traditional Routes- while they may seem like the last ditch and what all those other business plans might need to consider let me assure you most companies in my opinion will run this entire gauntlet to raise adequate funding and they should.
Friends & Family still make up the largest funding source for this non-traditional funding section. New innovations such as Micro-banking by firms such as ACCION

http://www.accionusa.org/home/support-u.s.-microfinance/learn-about-u.s.-microfinance/about-u.s.-microfinance.aspx and crowd funding through web based portals such as Crowdfunding Bank and Microventures.com are new waves in the highly mobile and interconnected society of today looking for low cost entry points and maximum flexibility and viral marketing exposure.

http://crowdfundingbank.com/
http://www.microventures.com/home?m=gooland2

Recommended Additional Reading:

There are a whole host of links to those of you who want to do your own sleuthing on this and feel you can run this gauntlet on your own without some professional advice and/or direction:

What Your State has to offer a guide to State & Local Incentives for Businesses?

http://business.usa.gov/stateandlocal?state

Site Location Considerations, something I was intricately involved in assisting in the development of an agreed upon approach for site location considerations:

http://www.iedconline.org/?p=data_standards

Local Real Estate Information Reports:

http://www.reis.com/index.cfm

Business Plans and Business Forms:

http://www.growthink.com/businessplan?&utm_source=google&utm_medium=cpc&utm_term=grow%20think&utm_

Incorporation for your entity is important in my opinion and I like Rocket Lawyer for turnkey services:

http://www.rocketlawyer.com/

The Federal Government is a great resource for both traditional and non-traditional financial information. You can visit the United Stated Small Business Administration website at http://www.sba.gov/

Professional Services Offered by the Author to Businesses

With our service that my firm offers, I walk you and your business through the landscape of opportunities, that, I feel might address your own unique business capital needs based on your custom response to our questionnaire. This could save you time and frustration in the pursuit of capitalization. There is something to be said for professional experience in these matters.

<u>Purchase your unique customized Business Case Opinion Today.</u> You will also receive a Consultation and SWOT analysis with your purchase of $99.95 by me. I will personally respond to your Business Question Survey based on my opinion of my recommended next steps to finalize your capitalization outreach after I have reviewed your information provided via our email template that will be sent to you once you make your purchase. Once you return your questionnaire and attach your business plan if you have one and any supporting material, I will contact you via email to establish a consultation via the telephone.

You may reach me via email at don.holbrook@economicdeveloper.com each additional consultation period thereafter is billed at $49.95 per 15-minute session and pre-authorized with each client in advance. You will not be billed additionally unless you request an additional consultation and there is no additional obligation to purchase anything. Every Initial purchase of $99.95 gets my "Art of the Deal Today" publication download once your purchase is approved as our gift to you as our new client. To make your purchase go to www.economicdeveloper.com/ click on business consulting services for your initial consultation package.

Disclosure Notice & Disclaimer:

The information I am providing is available via public domain. I have simply organized it and given you my professional overview of how it might be applied to your potential financing needs. Each business is unique and therefore there can be no guarantee of funding given nor is it implied by purchasing this product that you will achieve funding, furthermore even if you follow my professional advice after your consultation there is no assurance and/or guarantee that you will achieve your desired funding being sought. Developing relationships with investors and lenders is always a personal decision and professional decision by those involved that is beyond the control of our firm. It is understood by the client that Economic Developer LLC shall serve solely in the capacity of consultant and that Economic Developer LLC will not render any "expert" opinions and does not hold itself out as an "expert" (as the term "expert" is defined in Section 11 of the Securities Act of 1933).

Performance Based Consulting Representation by the Author (is not guaranteed):

If your project is within our normal guidelines of acceptable deal representation requirements and upon your request once your interview is concluded, we will email you our _"Performance Based Consultation Representation Proposal"_ that will enable our firm to assist you in finding the right capital sources for your project. Just like **our motto** says, *"If we don't find you your capital sources and assist you in closing on the necessary and acceptable capital you need for your business... we don't get paid."*

Our Fees are based on our standard rates of 3% of gross capital attained from the close escrow and 5% of any business incentives we negotiate on your behalf from any economic development or related public sector and/or quasi public sector agencies on your behalf. The value is based upon the cumulative value of the following types of public sector incentives, any agreement that lowers, avoids/abates/rebates, and/or defers any initial and/or on-going business costs that would have been applicable on the business in the jurisdictional area of operation and where the business enterprise is operated. These values are based upon the time line identified in the jurisdictional MOU between the client and the appropriate granting organization. We have a <u>no-refund policy</u> once the initial SWOT and business plan recommendations are given to our clients. Each business plan opinion is unique consulting work and requires time in preparation. Therefore on average you will receive a confirmation of receipt of your materials email and the initial telephone conversation normally will be scheduled within 5 business days of receipt of your payment. Your Written SWOT and Business Plan opinion and Next Step Recommendations will be sent within 2 business days after your telephone interview is concluded.

Here are the Questions that are typically needed for the business to answer prior to your consultation for economic development oriented capitalization consideration:

Your Name: Your Title:

Company Name:

Address:

City: State/Province:

Zip/Postal code:

Country:

What Type of Industry is Your Business in?

Your Major Products/Services:

Years of Operation/Year Incorporated/Established:

Gross Sales Last Fiscal Year:

Number of Employees:

Amount of Capital Being Sought:

Primary Use of Capital Sought:

For-Profit Business Structure: (LLC. Inc., Partnership, etc.)

Amount of Existing Equity Invested by owners $USD:

Amount of Existing Debt of the Business $USD:

Does your company sell products and/or services outside of your local region/community: (Yes or No)

Does your company currently Import products or raw materials from outside of North America: (Yes or no)

Does your company currently export any products or sell services internationally: (Yes or No)

Do you currently have a business plan: (Yes or no)

Do you currently have a business or personal line of credit available even if it is not sufficient for your business capitalization needs being sought: (Yes or No)

Do you have a current Financial Report/Statement: (Yes or no)

Do you currently have a formal private placement memorandum for soliciting investors: (Yes or no)

Do you currently have a market and/or product feasibility study that demonstrates the need for your investment in your targeted market? (Yes or no)

How large of a Facility does your business currently utilize for your business operations: (Square footage) _____?

Does this project require new construction? (Yes or no)

How large of a tract of land is minimum size acceptable in acres or percentage of an acre _____?

Will this investment of capital be used to increase the size and/or build an additional or new facility: (Yes or no)

If so, how large of a new Facility will this capital be used to expand and/or construct new: (square footage) _____?

What type of zoning or business area would your project typically best be located within (pick the most appropriate)

    __Office/Commercial Space

    __Retail/Shopping/Entertainment District

    __Industrial/Manufacturing

    __Warehouse/distribution

    __ Airport/Water Port

    __ Industry Park

How many jobs will this new investment generate within the jurisdiction, where the capital is going to be utilized in total _____?

Average Payroll Anticipated/# of Jobs anticipated per category:

- Low Skills- mostly manual labor ____?
- Semi-skilled workers with high productivity and some specialized skills ____?
- Office/Clerical Workers _____?
- Sales/Marketing/Management _____?
- Research/Technical Expertise with High Skill Levels _____?

Will this Capital be used for any of the following purposes: (pick the most appropriate)

- _____Expansion of existing facilities, new equipment and updated products/services

- _____Expansion into a new location to increase our business in a new region

- _____Relocation to a new area to lower our operating costs and better address market opportunities.

- _____This will be a brand new enterprise and will be built custom to our needs from a turn-key start-up basis

- _____This is a brand new enterprise but our company has been in business for many years and this is an expansion into additional new products and services for us.

- _____This is a new innovative concept that we feel is undervalued or not represented within our market and thus represents a tremendous high growth opportunity for potential investors

Glossary of Useful Economic Development Terms:

I am especially grateful to the International Economic Development Council (IEDC) and the California Association for Local Economic Development, CALED for creating the following useful glossary of economic development terms. For more information about IEDC, visit the following websites: www.iedconline.org and for CALED visit www.caled.org

Angel Investor... is an investor who providers equity investment to start-up businesses.

Assessed Valuation... the monetary worth of a property for the purposes of taxation. Total assessed valuation denotes the sum of the monetary worth of all taxable properties within a jurisdiction.

Backward and forward linkages... economic connections among companies; backward linkages involve the purchase of inputs by a given firm from another, and forward linkages involve the sale of the given firm's outputs to another company.

Base Industry... also known as "export" or "primary" industries, base industries sell or export their products and services outside the community and bring new dollars into the community, increasing the total dollars that circulate within the community and that are spent on non-base industries.

Benchmarking... definitive and quantifiable measures of economic competitiveness and quality of life that can be collected on a regular basis. They are used to measure a region's economic status and progress against comparable regions.

Bond... is a certificate of debt issued by a government or corporation guaranteeing payment of the original investment plus interest by a specified future date.

Brownfields... are commercial or industrial sites that are abandoned or under-utilized and have real or perceived environmental contamination.

Business Assistance Center... is a one-stop center for streamlining local permitting, licensing, and fee payment processes and facilitating the decision-making processes.

Business Attraction... the efforts by local economic development organizations to encourage firms from outside their communities to locate headquarters or other operations within their jurisdictions.

Business Climate... is the over-all environment of a given community that is relevant to the operation of a business; usually includes tax rates, attitudes of government toward business, and workforce availability. This creates an over-all cost of operation that is either healthy or not from the perspective of operational profitability.

Business Creation... is the economic development strategy that focuses on encouraging the formation of new companies that are locally based and will remain in the community and grow.

Business Incubator... is an entity that nurtures and supports young companies until they become viable, providing them with affordable space, technical and management support, equity and long-term debt financing, and employment. The three basic objectives in creating an incubator are (1) to spur technology-based development; (2) to diversify the local economy; and (3) to assist in community revitalization.

Business Improvement Districts (BIDS)... these are legally defined entities formed by property and business owners, where an assessment or a tax is levied for capital or operating improvements, as a means of supplementing city funding. The district is created by the public law or ordinance but is administered by an entity responsible to the district's members or to the local governing body. Some states authorize non-governmental, non-profit corporations. Recent BID programs include economic and social development, transportation, parking management, and conversion of redeveloped commercial buildings for residential use.

Business Recruitment and Attraction... is the traditional approach to economic development to entice companies to relocate or to set up a new branch plant or operation in a state or locality; often referred to as "smokestack chasing." This is the ultimate holy grail for economic developers... they want to claim the trophy and announce new businesses that are coming to their area, partly to give their political supporters something to ballyhoo about.

Business Retention... is the systematic effort designed to keep local companies content at their present locations which includes helping companies cope with changing economic conditions and internal company problems. Often this is the most overlooked area of responsibility for most economic development organizations.

CBD... is the central business district of a locality. Usually this is an area with the highest concentration of businesses, including financial institutions, shops, offices, theaters, and restaurants.

CDBG (Community Development Block Grants)... is a system of unified block grants under which communities with more than 50,00 people are entitled to receive funding while other communities may apply for discretionary funding. Its purpose is to encourage more broadly conceived community development projects and expand housing opportunities for low- and moderate-income persons. The three primary goals of CDBG are to serve low- and moderate-income people, to eliminate slums and blight, and to address other community development needs that pose a serious and immediate threat to the health and welfare of the community. This program has provided significant support for economic development projects.

CDC (Community Development Corporation)... are organizations, typically non-profit 501 (c) (3)s, which can obtain federal and private support. They are governed by local residents, businesses, and community leaders through a board of directors that is in most cases elected from the CDC membership or the community. Some CDCs perform only economic development services, but most work only on housing issues. Those active in economic development provide technical assistance and financing and are committed to serving the impoverished people of America.

CDC (Bank CDC)... are bank-sponsored community development corporations that are a way for banks to contribute to economic revitalization by investing in local businesses and real estate investment projects that benefit low- and moderate-income groups. A community can establish a bank CDC by working with one or more local banks, the Federal Reserve, the Comptroller, and its respective state financial institutions' regulators. In the case of consortium bank CDCs, where several banks join together, the investors do not have to be just local banks. Bank CDCs can purchase, construct, or rehabilitate property.

CDC (Certified Development Company)... is the originating and administrating body for the SBA 504 loans. The program provides long-term, fixed-rate financing to small businesses to acquire real estate, machinery, and equipment for the expansion of business or modernization of facilities. These organizations are normally independent but have good strong banking network relationships. The largest CDC is in San Diego, CA and serves California, Arizona and Nevada.

CDFI (Community Development Financial Institution)... is a specialized financial institution which works in market niches that have not been adequately served by traditional financial institutions. CDFIs provide a wide range of financial products and services, including mortgage financing, commercial loans, financing for community facilities, and financial services needed by low-income households. Some CDFIs also provide technical assistance. To be certified as a CDFI by the CDFI Fund of the Department of the Treasury, an institution must engage in community development, serve a targeted population, provide financing, have community representatives on its board, and be a non-governmental organization.

Capacity Building... is developing the ability of a community-based neighborhood organization to effectively design economic development strategies through technical assistance, networks, conferences, and workshops.

CAVE people- these are people within the community that oppose anything that is brought before any jurisdictional body for a public decision. CAVE stands for "Citizens Against Virtually Everything."

Certified and Preferred Lenders Program...U.S. Small Business Administration program that encourages highly active and expert lenders to provide funds to borrowers through a special designation of their internal ability to process and approve loans acceptable to the SBA..

Certified Development Company...(see CDC)

Clawbacks... as many localities enter into contracts requiring local commitments of capital from the public sector with private firms to which the public sector offers economic incentives for private sector investment, they create provisions for surety of performance or not. Clawbacks describe the punitive steps taken against firms that break these contracts. For example, a firm may be required to pay fines or assist in finding anew tenant for its property if it chooses to leave a community.

Clusters... a collocation of firms in the same or similar industries to foster interaction as a means of strengthening each other and enhancing the community's competitive advantage.

Community Development Venture Capital... is capital made available through funds created by local communities for the purpose of making venture capital accessible to entrepreneurs in low-income areas.

Comparative Advantage... is the term used when comparing economies of regions. It is the economic advantage gained by one area over another due to the fact that it can produce a particular product more efficiently. More efficient production of one good means there is a higher opportunity cost to produce another. This is the concept that drives trade between economies. Inter-regional and international trade exploits the comparative advantages of economies. (See Absolute Advantage)

Consolidated Plan... is the Consolidated Plan, or ConPlan, combines all of the planning, application, and performance requirements previously required separately for Community Development Block Grants (CDBG), HOME, Emergency Shelter Grants (ESG), Housing Opportunities for People with AIDS (HOPWA), and programs, such as HOME, that require a Comprehensive Housing Affordability Strategy (CHAS).

Corporate Welfare...is when the government subsidies targeted to large corporations create an artificial cost advantage that many in the general public and press may perceive as unnecessary.

Cost-Benefit Analysis... is a method for evaluating the profitability of alternative uses of resources and creating a hierarchy of best choices.

Cost Effective Analysis...compares the alternative projects or plans to determine the least costly way to achieve desired goals. Usually, some index or point system is developed to measure the effectiveness of the proposal in meeting the goals and objectives.

Customized Training...learning designed to meet the needs of a given employer; used by local governments to attract or retain major employers.

Demand-side Theory of Development... is the explanation of economic development that focuses on discovering, expanding, and creating new markets; forming new businesses; nurturing indigenous re-sources; and involving government in the economy.

DDA Difficult to Develop Areas- specially designated census tracts that receive more favorable consideration for federal and also state economic development funds, tax credits and loan programs as the area is either very rural or has a greater than average poverty rate and/or unemployment rate.

Eco-Industrial Park...is an industrial park designed to encourage business interaction in ways that foster the reuse of waste streams, the recycling of inputs, and other mechanisms that reduce the impact on the environment by using business affordable measures designed from the onset.

Economic Base... is a method of classifying all productive activity into two categories: basic industries which produce and sell goods that bring in new income from outside the area and service industries which produce and sell goods that simply circulate exiting income in the area.

Economic Base Analysis...is a comprehensive study of a locality's economy, focusing on the importance of exports. It should include an economic history, data on existing industries, trends, and forecasts of growth in wages and employment.

Economic Development Administration (EDA)... was created by the Public Works and Economic Act of 1965 as a part of the Commerce Department. The EDA's main goals are to alleviate unemployment and diversify the economy as well as assist urban areas with planning and emergency public works programs. It has been a highly controversial agency from Congress's view almost since it's inception.

Econometric Modeling... is a qualitative method for analyzing the impact of a proposed action on the economy. A model permits testing the effects of an anticipated or hypothetical change.

Economies of Scale... is the phenomenon of production where the average cost of production declines as more of the product is produced.

Edge City...is a newly emerged city that serves as a work and shopping center, with a large amount of office and retail space.

Eminent Domain...is the authority to "take" private property upon paying a fair price for the property and relocating the tenants. The most frequent use of this authority is the act of "condemnation." Recently this practice has come under huge media and general public scrutiny.

Empowerment Zones/Enterprise Communities (EZ/EC) Initiative... they were established in 1994 and are administered by the Department of Housing and Urban Development and Department of Agriculture, the federal EZ/EC tools include not only business tax incentives but also transportation to work or school, drug and alcohol rehabilitation, and other local priorities. The program creates incentives for localities to develop their own approaches to alleviate poverty. All federally designated zones are areas of pervasive poverty, unemployment, and general distress. Each designated city receives a mix of grants and tax-exempt bonding, while employers in the EZ/EC receive tax credits for new hires and accelerated depreciation credits.

Enterprise Development...is the assistance to entrepreneurs in support of the creation, growth, and survival of their businesses.

Enterprise Zones... are state enterprise zones that are designated geographic areas that are eligible for special treatment and incentives to attract private investment. State guidelines define the size of a zone and the minimum level of economic distress to qualify as an enterprise zone. States can also limit the number and type of enterprise zones. These restrictions are generally set out in the state enterprise zone program.

Entitlement Community...an entitlement community is eligible to receive annual CDBG funds that it can use to revitalize neighborhoods, expand affordable housing and economic opportunities, and/or improve community facilities and services, principally to benefit low- and moderate-income persons. Eligible grantees include local governments with 50,000 or more residents, other local governments designated as central cities of metropolitan areas, and urban counties with populations of at least 200,000 (excluding the population of entitled cities). The State CDBG Program offers funds to the state, which they then allocate among localities that do not qualify as entitlement communities.

Entrepreneurial Training... are programs that provide guidance and instruction on business basics such as accounting and financing to ensure that new businesses improve their chance of success. The most common training methods include classroom training, workshops, speakers, peer groups and one-on-one counseling, lectures, internships, as well as self-study and home-study.

Equity Financing... are investments that are typically secured in this type of financial support in return for partial ownership of an enterprise; three mechanisms can be used for receiving an equity position in a firm: common stock, preferred stock, and convertible debt.

First Wave... the strategic paradigm of economic development that focuses on business attraction tactics as a primary catalyst to revitalize or maintain an economic vitality.

Fiscal Impacts...is the direct and indirect costs incurred and revenues received by local governments resulting from land use and other types of decision.

501(c)(3)...approval given by the Internal Revenue Service granting exemption from federal income tax to a nonprofit organization, under Section 501(c)(3) of the Internal Revenue Code. Donations to such organizations are tax deductible. The organizations described in 501(c)(3) are commonly referred to under the general heading "charitable organizations."

501(c)(6)...approval given by the Internal Revenue Service granting exemption from federal income tax to a business league, under Section 501(c)(6) of the Internal Revenue Code. Trade Associations and professional associations are considered to be business leagues. The business league must be devoted to the improvement of business conditions of one or more lines of business as distinguished from the performance of particular services for individual persons. No part of its net earnings may inure to the benefit of any private shareholder or individual and it may not be organized for profit or organized to engage in an activity ordinarily carried on for profit.

Gap Financing...is a loan required by a developer to bridge the gap, i.e. to make up a deficiency be-tween the amount of mortgage loan due upon project completion and the expenses incurred during construction (financing that covers the difference between what a project can support and the cost of development or purchase).

General Obligation (G.O.) Bonds... are the traditional form of borrowing for state and local government; se-cured by full faith and credit of jurisdiction.

Limited Tax G.O. Bonds... are tax-exempt bonds secured by the revenue from the application of a fixed rate against taxable property. Not all states permit limited tax G.O.s, but in those that do, such bond issuance does not require voter approval.

Unlimited Tax G.O. Bonds... are tax-exempt bonds secured through taxes that are levied without rate or amount limitations in order to repay the principal and interest of the bond. They are typically used to finance public works infrastructure and land acquisition for blight elimination.

Impact Fees...are fees that are required to cover costs of improving and/or building infrastructure needed as a result of the expected impact of development project on those facilities. Often required by localities for the approval of development projects. These can be negotiated prior to development in many cases by the site location consultant to reduce costs to the business owners.

Incentives...any economic benefits offered to firms as part of an business attraction strategy that will create jobs, tax base and/or improve the diversification and economic development goals of an area. A few incentives are tax abatements and credits, low interest loans, infrastructure improvements, job training, and land grants, interest buy downs, turnkey leaseback build to suit facilities, debt participation or conduit financing options.

Incubator-Without-Walls... is a form of business incubation that does not take place in a single building, but instead comprises a network of entrepreneurs and entrepreneurship service providers throughout a community or region.

Industrial Development Bonds...these bonds are used to finance acquisition, construction, expansion, or renovation of manufacturing facilities and the purchase of machinery and equipment depending upon state law. IDB financing is subject to state and local laws and federal income tax laws and regulations if the interest on the bonds is expected to be exempt from federal income taxation.

Industrial Revenue Bonds...bonds that provide lower-cost financing for real property improvements or the purchase or construction of buildings, facilities, or equipment.

Industry Clusters... are geographic concentrations of related businesses B complementary or competing. Regions identify clusters as targeted businesses for future planning and marketing efforts. There are two types: (1) buyer-supplier clusters and (2) shared resources clusters.

Infrastructure Banks...are public-targeted lending facilities, financed through a combination of bond issues, government funds and external donor support. They mobilize domestic funds, and create an at-tractive vehicle for donor funding.

Investor Networks...are investor networks that match up potential investors (either anonymous "angel" investors or know investors) with start-up firms needing capital as a matchmaking opportunity.

Land Banking...is a program that preserves

industrial/commercial space for a city. A city or local development authority acquires and holds land until a developer steps forward with a proposal for its use as an industrial/commercial applicable site use plan.

Jobs-Housing Imbalance... is the spatial mismatch between where people live and where they work.

Just-in-Time Inventorying... are cost-saving approaches by a manufacturer that involves maintaining no inventory of product inputs on-site; instead the inputs are delivered from the supplier(s) at the time they are needed in the production process.

Labor-Force Theory of Development...is the explanation of development that stresses the importance of an educated, skilled, and dependable workforce for attracting and growing businesses; accepts the concept that the public sector has a responsibility to fit human resources to the needs of the business community.

Land Write-Down....is providing land to developers at a price that is below public sector expenses for improvements in order to incentivize their action to construct a project.

Loan Pooling...is when two or more lenders contribute to a fund from which loans are made to applicants; publicly chartered, privately funded corporations can be established to pool resources.

Location Theory of Development...is the explanation of economic development that emphasizes factors such as transportation, access to raw materials and labor, taxes, business climate, and quality of life as they relate to industrial location.

Long-Wave Theory of Development...is an explanation of economic development that contends that bursts of innovation lead to economic growth and long-term economic windfalls.

Mezzanine Capital...are the funds or goods used to bridge the gap in resources from one stage of business to another. (See also Gap Financing)

Microenterprise... is a business that is "smaller-than-small." Operated by a person on a full- or part-time basis, usually out of a home, e.g., carpenters, day-care providers, and caterers.

Microloans... are very small, short-term unsecured loans given to people without credit history and/or the collateral necessary to obtain a conventional loan. These are available from either local lenders or the SBA's 7(m) Microloan Program.

Minority Businesses Development Agency (MBDA)... is an agency with the U.S. Department of Commerce, MBDA was established in 1969. The MBDA Provides assistance to socially- or economically-disadvantaged individuals who own or want to start a business. MBDA provides funding for Minority Business Development Centers, Native American Business Development Centers, Business Resource Centers, and Minority Business Opportunity Committees.

Moderate Income... is a definition based on family income as a percentage of an area's median income. Different programs may set different percentages. According to HUD's guidelines, households whose incomes are between 81 percent and 95 percent of an area's median income with adjustments for smaller or larger families are considered to be moderate income.

Multiplier... is a quantitative estimate of a project's impact (in dollars, jobs created, demand).

Multiplier Effect... the process of dollar and job generation as a result of a new or migrating business or project, or of a local business expanding production (to exports). The multiplier effect accounts for new local income generated by local spending that came from outside a community.

NIMBY ("Not in My Backyard")... is a common term used to describe local opposition to development projects and is very prevalent in most communities as the vocal minority of citizenry that are very focused on government decision making in general.

North American Development Bank...was founded under the auspices of the North American Free Trade Agreement (NAFTA), NADB is a "bilaterally-funded, international organization, in which Mexico and the United States participate as equal partners." Its purpose is to finance environmental infrastructure projects. All financed environmental projects must be certified by the Border Environment Cooperation Commission, be related to potable water supply, wastewater treatment or municipal solid waste management and be located in the border region.

North American Industry Classification System (NAICS)... is the industrial classification code system used for categorizing industrial establishments. Beginning in 1997, NAICS replaced the Standard Industrial Classification (SIC) as the system for classifying firms in the United States, Canada, and Mexico.

One-Stop Business Service Centers...are One-stop business service centers are facilities where business persons can go to obtain the licenses and permits needed to start-up, operate, and expand their facilities. These centers improve the local business environment while reducing the number of separate agencies and offices a business must apply to for various licenses and permits, saving public and private time and financial resources.

Opportunity Cost...is the revenue forgone by choosing one use of money and resources over another. The opportunity cost of investing in the stock market is the interest that the money could have earned while sitting in the bank.

Overall Economic Development Plan (OEDP)... a plan developed at the city, county or EDD level, as required by EDA, to identify the area's problems & opportunities for economic development, to de-fine goals & objectives, and listing infrastructure & other projects needed to achieve those goals.

Revenue Bond...is a bond backed by anticipated revenue stream from specific project and it can be public or private sector in nature in most cases. New innovate uses are Sales Tax

Anticipated Revenue bond sales (STAR) bonds used for development that will produce large retail sales tax streams of revenues. This is basically a form of Tax Increment Financing (TIF).

Revolving Loan Fund (RLF)...is a pool of public and private sector funds in which the money is recycled to make successive loans to businesses. Loans made by an RLF are repaid with interest and the payment are returned to replenish the lending pool so new loans can be made. The funds are thus recycled and the RLF grows as each generation of borrowers adds to the pool.

Seed Capital...is any equity money supplied to help a company get off the ground. The money is almost always supplied by an entrepreneur and his/her family, friends, and relatives. Used to help attract (leverage) other investment.

Second Wave...is the strategic paradigm of economic development that focuses on retaining firms already in the community and on creating new businesses.

Secondary Financing...is a loan secured by a second mortgage on a property, sometimes used to refer to any financing techniques other than equity and first-mortgage debt. We most often refer to this as subordinated debt financing.

Shift-Share Analysis...is a method used to examine a local area's basic industries in terms of their growth and decline relative to national or regional trends.

Site Location Assistance...is the process where local governments compete to provide new, expanding, and relocating businesses with assistance and economic incentives for locating the sites and/or their business operations, which fit their facility's needs in the community. These services include provide information on sites, community demographics, business costs, workforce benefits and the organized unionization of the workforce if any along with business infrastructure and logistics of transportation options and the organizing of visitation programs for potential new businesses. Site Location

Consultants are experts at creating the most favorable terms for the business owner to make the best choice for their business location and most cost-effective use of capital for such purposes.

Small Business Administration (SBA)...founded in 1953, SBA's mission is to "aid, counsel, assist and protect, insofar as is possible, the interests of small business concerns." Its charter also mandates that the SBA ensure small businesses a "fair proportion" of government contracts and sales of surplus property. Since its inception, the SBA has delivered more than 13 million loans, loan guarantees, con-tracts, and other form of assistance to small businesses.

Small Business Development Center (SBDC)...facility that provides business development, information, and assistance in one location; administered by the U.S. Small Business Administration.

Small Business Investment Company (SBIC)...privately owned and managed for-profit investment firms that use their own capital, plus funds borrowed at favorable rates with an SBA guarantee, to make venture capital investments in small businesses.

Smart Growth...the efficient use of all available assets. According to the American Planning Association, smart growth involves efficient land use; full use of urban services; mixed use; mass transportation options; and detailed, human-scaled design.

Smokestack Chasing...is a term used to describe the pursuit of traditional manufacturing businesses by local economic development organizations.

Social Capital...is in economic development, the linkages between and among business development service providers and the companies they assist; these linkages are both internal, within a given-service provider organization, and external, between an organization (and its clients) and external service providers and businesses.

Special Assessment Districts...are areas designated by a taxing authority to be assessed for tax purposes on a scale that differs from the rest of the taxed jurisdiction. Property in these districts may be taxed differently all together. They may be required to pay special taxes more reflective of the greater benefit earned by some public expenditure in the district.

Special Assessment Funds...are the costs of a project that benefit a specific group of properties may be assessed to those individuals and accounted for in the special assessment fund.

Special Improvement Districts...are local government mechanisms where local businesses and/or residents agree to voluntarily pay an additional tax to support improvements or services so local governments can finance and implement improvements within a specific and limited area. (Similar to Business Improvement Districts)

Start-Up...is a company in the first stage of the evolution of a business.

Start-Up Capital...are the required funds that help nascent enterprises acquire space, equipment, supplies, and other inputs needed to launch a business.

Supply-Side Theory of Development...is an explanation of economic development that focuses on reducing costs of production to lure capital to a new location; typical strategies include tax abatements, reductions, and exemptions; guaranteed and direct loans; and reduced regulation.

Sustainable Development...is the development that does not destroy or eventually deplete a location's natural resources. Sustainable development helps ensure a better, healthier living environment and contributes to an area's quality of life, one of the main goals of economic development.

SWOT Analysis... is a tool used in the economic development planning process to assess a community's Strengths and Weaknesses, factors from within a community that can be changed, as well as its Opportunities and Threats, factors from outside that cannot be changed. Businesses can use this term for their own assessment of their current business situation.

Tax Abatement...is the exemption or reduction of local taxes of a project for a specific period of time. Contracts between a government entity and a holder of real estate that stipulate that some share of assessed value will not be taxed for an agreed time period; a typical goal of tax abatement is to encourage economic development.

Tax Credit...are monies directly subtracted from a tax bill after a tax liability has been incurred that can reduce the cost of capital.

Tax Deferral...is a policy that permits individuals whose property values have risen dramatically through no fault of their own to pay taxes on the basis of old values.

Tax -Exempt Bond...is an debt obligation instrument that does not require recipients of interest payments to pay taxes on the interest revenue; although revenue bonds may be a form of tax-exempt bonds, not all revenue bonds qualify for a tax exemption (e.g., stadium projects, parking facilities, and non-government office buildings lost their tax-exempt status in 1986).

Tax Exemption...is the policy that reduces the base form which property is assessed; accomplished by subtracting a given amount of money from the assessed market rate. Tax exemptions are often granted to individuals, institutions, or types of property.

Tax Incentives...are the use of various tax relief measures such as tax exemptions, tax credits or tax abatements to recruit and attract businesses to a community or help local businesses expand.

Tax Increment Financing (TIF)...a common practice finance tool of economic development in which taxes that can be traced to a specific development are used to repay bonds that were issued to finance some portion of that development. When bonds are fully paid, the jurisdiction can begin to receive the additional tax revenue produced by the development and/or in some cases pool those unrestricted proceeds for future project funding consideration.

Tax Stabilization Agreement...is an agreement to not raise taxes significantly; used to assure potential investors of a stable tax environment.

Technical Assistance... are services that include aid with preparing grant applications, training staff, applying for loans and marketing the product. It may also include assisting a small business to improve its product or manufacturing process. Technical assistance is generally aimed at providing specific services that a small business typically cannot afford, or general business planning.

Third Wave...is a strategic paradigm of economic development that aims to create a local or regional environment that is supportive of growth and development.

Thrivival- is the term coined by author Don A. Holbrook in his book series that defines the constant evolving process of individuals, communities and companies learning to constantly adapt to change and learning to thrive in a constant landscape of economic uncertainty while in a mode of destructive learning which, is the development of a survival mindset. Frequently called finding pearls of opportunity in times of great economic chaos and/or uncertainty.

Under employed...includes all persons whose skills, education or training qualified them for a higher skilled or better paying job than they presently hold. It also includes persons only able to find part-time rather than full-time work in their fields.

Umbrella Bonds...are low-cost financing with lower interest rates for projects too small to qualify for normal revenue bond programs. Bond proceeds are used as loans for acquisition of land, building, machinery, and equipment. The umbrella is a pool of small bonds of $1 million or less packaged into a larger bond and issued by the state or local economic development agency.

Unemployed...are those people in the workforce that are defined by the U.S. Department of Labor, as all civilians who were not employed, but were available and actively seeking work within the past four weeks, were waiting to be called back to a job from which they had been laid off, or were waiting to report to a new job scheduled to begin within 30 days.

Value-Added...is Revenue created by the processing of resources; the amount of revenue is greater be-cause those resources have been processed.

Venture Capital...is an investment made where there is a possibility of very substantial returns on the investment, as much as 40 percent, within a short period. It is usually invested in dynamic, growing, and developing enterprises, not in start-ups.

Workforce Investment Act...Workforce Investment Act of 1998 is the federal government's effort to adapt workforce training system to current economic conditions. The economic development impact of WIA includes: (1) decentralizing decision-making to the local level; (2) allows local businesses to determine skill needs; (3) adapt training to local growth patterns; (4) promotes inclusion of economic development principles in plans; and (5) state required to submit economic development plans with WIA implementation plan.

List of Most Typically Used Financial Terms

Bond- A certificate of debt issued to raise funds. Bonds typically pay a fixed rate of interest and are repayable at a fixed date.

Capital Budgeting- The process of managing capital assets and planning future expenditure on capital assets

Capital Investments- Funds invested by a business in its capital assets that are anticipated to be used before being replaced. Capital investments are generally significant business expenses, requiring long-term

Current Assets- A balance sheet item, current assets are those items owned by the firm with the intention to generate profits or other assets that can be converted to cash within one year. It includes cash, account receivables, inventory, cash equivalents and other cash equivalents.

Convertible Loans- A loan with a provision allowing it to be converted to equity within a specific

Convertible Preferred Shares- Preference equity shares issued by a business that includes a provision allowing them to be converted to ordinary equity shares after a specific time frame.

Creditor/Accounts Payable- Suppliers the company owes money to, usually for services or goods supplied.

Creditors Turn-over Rate- A short-term liquidity measure used to quantify the rate at which a business pays

Debt Financing/Accounts Receivable- The money that you borrow to finance a business. Customers who owe the company money, usually for services or goods supplied

Debtor Turn-over Rate- A short-term liquidity measure used to quantify the rate at which a business receives

Default Risk- The risk of loss due to non-payment by the borrower.

EBITDA- The earnings before interest, taxes, depreciation and amortization. It is the net cash inflow from operating activities, before working capital requirements are taken into account.

EBITDA Margin- A measure of operating performance. It is calculated by dividing EBITDA by sales and is usually expressed as a percentage.

Equity Financing- The issuance of ordinary shares to raise money for a business

Factoring- The selling the interest in the accounts receivable or invoices to a financial institution at a small discount. It is sometimes called "accounts receivable financing".

Factoring helps a company speeds up its cash flow so that it can more readily pay its current obligations and grow.

Fixed Assets- Fixed assets are those long-term tangible assets that the business has acquired for use to earn income over more than one year. These assets normally must have a useful life over a few years and not expected to be converted to cash in the current financial year. Examples include, factory, warehouse, equipment

FF&E- a term used for the expression of the amount of Facilities, Fixtures and Equipment a business is utilizing, has in value or is going to purchase.

Convertible Debt- Monies that are loaned to a company that can be converted to equity at an agreed upon conversion of value ratio.

Blue Sky Laws- the rules applicable in each state as to how you can raise private capital from the solicitation of non-qualified investors (those people not of high wealth by definition) and qualified investors.

Initial Public Offering- The placement of availability of a company's stock for the first time on the private equity market.

Interest Coverage Ratio- An indication of the ability of a business to cover interest expenses with its income. It is calculated by dividing income before interest and taxes by interest paid.

Letter of Credit- A written assurance given by a bank and/or lending institution to another party that a specified amount of money is available for their guaranteed of providing some economic value for a specified time period.

Trust Receipt- A financing facility for imports where a bank makes an advance to the buyer to settle an import sight bill. The advance is generally for a certain period. On the due date, the buyer is required to settle the bill with interest at an agreed rate.

Profit Margin- A measure of a company's profitability. It is calculated by dividing net profit by sales and is usually expressed as a percentage

Private Placement Memorandum- An official document that states the business case for a private debt or equity investment into a business by investors, which states their risks for making the investment, intended uses of the funding and potential exit strategies or return of capital to the investor over a projected but not guaranteed timeline generally.

Operating Capital- The amount of capital required to pay for the annual cost of paying for raw materials, payroll, marketing and sales expense, debt, interest, taxes and delivery of services and products along with facilities costs, utilities, telephone, and maintenance on the premise.

Overhead- The annual cost of all operating costs that is necessary before profit is achieved.

Return on Equity- A measure of the return on each dollar of shareholder investment. It is calculated by dividing net profit by equity and is usually expressed as a percentage

Risk Capital- The amount of funds an investor is willing to put at risk of not being recovered from their disposable assets.

Seed Capital- The initial capital raised to fund a business or project getting commenced but not normally the full amount of necessary capital to bring the business or project to sustainable revenues.

Stock turnover- A measure of inventory performance to show how fast stock is converted from purchases to sales. It is calculated by dividing stock level by cost of sales x 365 days

Term Loan- A loan for a fixed period of more than one year and repayable by regular installments

Qualified Investor- A high net worth individual who generally has experience in investing in at-risk business ventures and who has a net worth over $1M in liquid assets and has an income in excess of $250K per year over the past 3 years prior to their investment in the current business venture.

Venture Capitalist- Someone who takes extremely higher than normal risks on new business ideas and companies prior to their realizing their market potential and sustainable value. These type individuals generally expect a very high return on investment in less than a 5 year time period of investment.

Don A. Holbrook, Certified Economic Development Finance Professional, CEcD, FM

Don Holbrook is a private consultant/practitioner involved in the major elements of economic development public policy financing strategies, site location analysis & business incentive development and negotiations with the public sector for business locations. He is considered as one of the fields most influential and recognized subject matter experts on the "Art of the Deal Today."

Holbrook is located in Las Vegas, NV. He has worked on a wide variety of projects representing billions of dollars in local economic impact and capital investment generating thousands of jobs in his 20+ years in the profession.

He has specialized in creating customized incentive policies such as equity funding, specialized tax increment funding & tax abatements concepts, workforce tax credits, specialized state legislation to increase equity and reduce operational costs in order to attract and finance projects, he is known for his creative hybrid capitalization development models. These investments by communities and other targeted incentives/business inducements reduce the over-all cost of the project to his clients and/or help his public sector clients close deals to attract the necessary project funding to projects in search of capitalization.

He has worked with economic organizations worldwide in developing strategic plans, core market assessment, target industry analysis, special business attraction incentive policies and the development of public backed strategic business investments in capital formation and permanent convertible subordinated debt financing. His focus is to create public-private partnerships that are built on real world economic realities tied to a well-balanced capabilities driven business model that rewards risk being taken by both public and private partners.

Holbrook is recognized for his prowess in the economic development industry as an early pioneer of site location and community-profiling online technology based infrastructure as well as assisted in establishing the data standards utilized by the IEDC today for site location analysis.

He is one of the most respected and renowned public speakers available on the topic of rebuilding local economies and finding hybrid capitalization for innovative projects. He speaks frequently on the topic of "The Art of the Deal Today" and "Surviving and Thriving in Today's Economic Turbulence." He has authored three books within the profession, "Who Moved My Smoke Stack" in 2008 and his first book, "The Little Black Book of Economic Development" released in 2007 is still a best seller in the economic development industry. His most recent book, published in 2011 is "The Next America-Moving Beyond a Fragile Economy." Holbrook is one of the most highly published and quoted subject matter experts in the field of economic development worldwide.

Index

www.ingramcontent.com/pod-product-compliance
Lightning Source LLC
Chambersburg PA
CBHW030817180526
45163CB00003B/1323